MW01008331

You Are...

31 DAILY D.R.O.P.'s OF HEALTHY THOUGHTS

EMERALD S. WADE

KP PUBLISHING COMPANY

ISBN: 978-1-950936-07-6 (Paperback)
ISBN: 978-1-950936-08-3 (Ebook)
Library of Congress Control Number: 2019907861

Edited by: Stephanie Struyck Elgin
Cover Design: Angie Alaya
Interior Design: Jennifer Houle
Library Director: Sandra L. Slayton

Published by:

KP Publishing Company
A Division of Knowledge Power Communications, Inc.
Valencia, CA 91355
www.kp-pub.com

Printed in the United States of America

31 D.R.O.P.'s

DEDICATION

To my beautiful mom, Christine Magana Nixon, who worked tirelessly to create my childhood grape costume and continues to go above and beyond. I love you. YOU ARE . . .

This book is dedicated to all you beautiful ladies-the young and the seasoned. This book is for every woman who has ever doubted her beauty or her worth; every woman who has ever compared herself to another woman; every woman who has ever put down another woman for being who she is and who you are not; every woman who has ever found herself in need of some self-love. These daily D.R.O.P.'s will allow you to be reminded of who you are. You may think that you do not have all of these attributes but I believe that you will have what you say and that ultimately, you are who God says you are. My prayer is that you will make time to meditate on these daily D.R.O.P.'s to the point that they will settle well with your spirit and you will begin to agree with who YOU ARE.

INTRODUCTION: 31 DAILY D.R.O.P.'s OF HEALTHY THOUGHTS

drop: (n) a small quantity of liquid that falls or is produced in a more or less spherical mass; a minute quantity of anything.

D.R.O.P.
Acronym for **D**efinition. **R**eflection. **O**bservation. **P**etition.

Here is what you will find in each **D.R.O.P.**:

Definition: Define the "Healthy Thought" by use of dictionary.com

Reflection: Reflect on what it is to be the "Healthy Thought" by way of scriptures and personal experience/ knowledge of the author.

Observation: Encourage the reader to look at themselves and see where they are personally with the "Healthy Thought."

Petition: Pray a simplified prayer that purposefully repeats the "Healthy Thought" for meditation.

When you think about a drop, often times a drop of water comes to mind. Though it is minute in nature, it has the ability to become a puddle if it continues to drip. This is the same way we can view our thoughts. One thought (drop) can start off small but if we continue to ponder whatever thought it may be, it has the potential to become a big puddle in our mind, causing us to feel overwhelmed.

Definition of overwhelm: (v) To overcome completely in mind or feeling.

Being overwhelmed is not necessarily negative. You can be overwhelmed with joy just as much as you can be overwhelmed with sadness—two very opposite feelings but both very tangible emotions based on our thoughts and our experiences. But with that being said, we have the power to shift the result of our experiences by the way we think. Ultimately, our thoughts have more power to affect our lives than our experiences ever will;

which we tend to like to give much credit to (our experiences) when it comes to us being who we are. But that is another conversation for another day or book.

In this book, you will find 31 Daily D.R.O.P.'s of Healthy Thoughts. You are encouraged to meditate on one D.R.O.P. per day. Each Daily D.R.O.P. is a slow yet healthy way for you to digest who you are. May this book allow you to begin (or continue) to think healthy about who You Are, one D.R.O.P. at a time.

Resources Used:
www.dictionary.com; www.biblegateway.com;
http://prayercentral.net/engage-me/ways-to-pray/pray-with
-acts/ (**A.C.T.S.: A**doration. **C**onfession. **T**hanksgiving.
Supplication. Format used for writing simplified Petitions)

D.R.O.P. #1

You Are...

LOVED

DEFINITION:

LOVED: (*adjective*) Held in deep affection; cherished.

REFLECTION:

Have you ever wondered what it would be like to be fully cherished? For someone to want to hold you so close? For someone to want to care for you so dearly; they just want to be around you all day?

For some that may be a little too much affection, but for others that may be just what the doctor ordered. Either way, did you know that this is how God feels about you? He wants to be so close to you that you and Him become one. The Bible says in

John 10:27, "My sheep hear My voice, and I know them, and they follow Me." It also says in James 4:8a, "Draw near to me and I will draw near to you." This is why I believe that God was confidently able to say that you were made in His image and in His likeness (Genesis 1:26). The more time you spend with Him the more that you will become like Him. It is inevitable!

When you spend a lot of time with someone, you will begin to know their voice and even take on some of their character traits. And in this case, when it comes to God, one of those traits is love. God is love. And because God is love, you too, are love. And because you are love, you also are loved. It may be a bit of a tongue twister way of thinking, but in a nutshell, the truth is YOU ARE LOVED.

OBSERVATION:
Take time to think of how you view yourself. The way that you carry yourself, allow others to treat you, etc., does it show that you know you are loved? The greatest commandment is written in Mark 12:30-31. It reads, "And you shall love the Lord your God with all your heart, with all your soul, with all your mind, and with all your strength." This is the first commandment. And similarly, the second, is this: "You shall love your neighbor as yourself. There is no other commandment greater than

these." How are you treating your neighbor? Believe it or not, but the truth is how you treat your neighbor is a direct reflection of how much you believe you are loved. Unforgiveness issues? Jealousy issues? Envy issues? Again, this is all a reflection of how you treat and love yourself. Think about it. Look at your life and see what it is saying about who you are in the area of being LOVED.

PETITION:

Dear Lord,

You are holy! Forgive me for not always believing that I am loved. Thank you for letting me know that I am loved. Help me to remember each day that I AM LOVED.

In Jesus' name, Amen.

D.R.O.P. #2

You Are...

IMPORTANT

DEFINITION:

IMPORTANT: (*adjective*) Of much or great significance or consequence; prominent or large.

REFLECTION:

What caught my eye about one of the definitions of "important" was the word "large." This immediately screamed out to me, "YOU ARE A BIG DEAL!" Think about it. To say that you are large is to say that you are a huge deal! You are of great importance! You matter! You have been created to take up space! The Bible reads in Genesis 1:26, "Then God said, 'Let us make man in our image, according to our likeness; let them have dominion over the fish of the sea, over the birds of the air, and over the cattle, over all the earth and over every creeping thing that creeps on the earth." If this scripture doesn't scream out to you that you are important, then I really do not know what else will.

God desires that you have dominion, that you take authority over all the things that He has entrusted to you. If you were not of great significance, then God would have never created you in the first place. You have been created for a purpose and for a specific destiny. Even if you are not certain of what exactly that is at this time, at least rest and move (yes, at the same time) in knowing that God has given you permission to be great, to make big moves, and again, to take up space! Don't take up space in a negative way like when people say, "Move out the way, you're taking up too much space," but rather a positive way. Take up space like you know you belong here. Take up space like this business cannot function without you. Take up space like you know you have the answer to the problem and you are going to solve it. Take up space like you know that you know that you know that YOU ARE IMPORTANT.

OBSERVATION:

Take time to think of how you view yourself. Do you carry yourself with an aura of importance or do you drag yourself around like no one cares about you? Have you been lied to about the fact that your existence is of essence? And has that lie come from someone you know, a stranger or even from yourself? Many people may say negative things about you, but ultimately you have the power to carry that thought through. Do not let the power of people's words outweigh the power of God's word. And His word says that you are important. Jeremiah 29:11 reads, "For I know the thoughts that I think toward you, says the Lord, thoughts of peace and not of evil, to give you a future and a hope." Only important people have a future and you, my dear, are one of them. Think about it. Look at your life and see what it is saying about who you are in the area of being IMPORTANT.

PETITION:
Dear Lord,

You are wonderful! Forgive me for not always believing that I am important. Thank you for letting me know that I am important. Help me to remember each day that I AM IMPORTANT.

In Jesus' name, Amen.

D.R.O.P. #3

You Are...

VALUABLE

DEFINITION:

VALUABLE: (*adjective*) having considerable monetary worth; costing or bringing a high price; having qualities worthy of respect, admiration, or esteem.

REFLECTION:

Have you ever settled for less because you felt like that was God's best for you? Have you ever allowed someone to defame you, manipulate you, abuse you, chastise you, because you felt like you could not do anything about your situation or because you simply did not care? Have you ever felt worthless? Have you ever walked around believing that you are unworthy of love, respect, admiration or high esteem?

This question reminds me of an old song by the singer Brandi titled "Have You Ever." The song went something like this, "Have you ever loved somebody so much it makes you cry? Have you ever needed someone so much you can't sleep at night? Have you ever tried to find the words but they don't come out right? Have you ever? Oh have you ever?" The song continues to speak about a love that she had for someone who did not have the same love for her in return. She had valued this person to the point of feeling hopeless that the person did not feel the same in return but still desired that one day he would. This reminds me of Proverbs 13:12. It reads, "Hope deferred makes the heart sick, But when the desire comes, it is a tree of life."

I remember having a crush on this one person for the longest of time. He did not feel the same way about me and it hurt. My hope in being his girl was denied and my heart broke. I felt that because he did not care for me like I had wanted him to, it meant that no one cared. Sometimes this is how it feels when you esteem someone higher than you should. You put them on a pedestal they were never meant to stand on. In essence, they become an idol; which, as you may know, is never good, because in the end you must know that your value does not come from someone else but rather from the Lord. Psalm

139:14 reads, "I will praise You, for I am fearfully and wonderfully made; marvelous are your works, and that my soul knows very well."

Does your soul know fully well that you are marvelous? Your soul is comprised of your mind, emotions, will, intellect and imagination. With that being said, imagine if your soul knew without a doubt that you were perfectly created. No one could persuade you to think any differently. This is how it must be. You must know that you are superb. You are of excellent quality. Think about it. You come from royalty. You are the child of the Most High God; a child of the King. You come from good stock. You are an extension of God's goodness. You are priceless. My dear one, YOU ARE VALUABLE.

OBSERVATION:

Take time to think of how you view yourself. Take a look at all of your relationships—relationships with family, friends, loved ones, etc. Assess how you have been treated and determine if the treatment is one that is of quality and respect or one of wasted time and dishonor. Think about it. Look at your life and see what it is saying about who you are in the area of being VALUABLE.

PETITION:

Dear Lord,

You are awesome! Forgive me for not always believing that I am valuable. Thank you for letting me know that I am valuable. Help me to remember each day that I AM VALUABLE.

In Jesus' name, Amen.

D.R.O.P. #4

You Are...

POWERFUL

DEFINITION:

POWERFUL: (*adjective*) having or exerting great power or force; physically strong, as a person.

REFLECTION:

Have you ever heard people say after watching a movie or hearing someone speak, "That was powerful?" I know for me, when I hear people say, "That was powerful," or when I say, "That was powerful," what I hear it to mean is that IT was impactful. It moved me. It caused me to think differently. It shifted my focus. It made me want to go out and be someone greater. It made me want to respect and honor that person more. It made me want to love more. It made me want to move into action. In essence, whatever "it" was caught one of my five senses and charged me to respond. The force behind what I saw, heard, touched, tasted and or smelled did something inside of me that made me want to move. There was a call to action.

Each of us have been called to do something great; to be someone great. Why? Because we have been "created for such a time as this." This is a phrase that is found in the book of Esther (4:14b). A quick backdrop, Queen Esther had found out through her cousin Mordecai, that her people (the Jews) were sentenced to be killed due to King Ahasuerus (Esther's husband) being told by his right-hand man, Haman, that the Jews did not keep the king's laws and so they needed to be destroyed. Mordecai heard the news and sent a message to Esther stating that she needed to approach the king and save her people. Mordecia expressed to Esther that she was called for such a time as this; basically meaning that perhaps this was the purpose as to why she became the wife to King Ahasuerus. Esther was now in the perfect position to move on it. The "it" for Queen Esther was to expose who she truly was to the king and believe God that the king would not kill her but love her to the point that he would put an end to the death sentence of her people. Esther ended up telling Mordecai to have all of their people fast (no eating or drinking) and pray along with her for three days and nights. They would do this leading to her day of action. In the end, Esther gained the strength to approach the king, and as a result, she was not killed and her people were saved. In fact, the only one who was put to death was Haman.

How awesome is it to know that you have the authority to make a difference? Just like Esther, you have the power to make big moves and to call big shots. You have the power to expose the devil and his lies by speaking the truth and walking in the truth. You have the power to shift an atmosphere by just being present and standing up tall using the authority that God has given you to cause the environment to change. You have the power to say yes and no to whatever may come your way. You have the power to decide what you will and will not stand for in your life. You have the power to say, "I do," to the one you have decided to marry and to make the marriage last until the end of time by walking in love. You have the power to be healed by proclaiming healing scriptures over your life and not wavering in faith. You have the power to change and be transformed by renewing your mind through the word of God. You have the power to do all these things and more because YOU ARE POWERFUL.

OBSERVATION:

Take time to think of how you view yourself. Do you see yourself as powerful? Do you see yourself as one who has the authority to make things happen? Do you know that in your weakness God is made strong? Do you know that the joy of the Lord is your strength? You see, you were never meant to do this life alone. You were always meant to walk this life out with Jesus Christ on your side. The Bible says in Hebrews 7:25, "Therefore He is also able to save to the uttermost those who come to God through Him, since He always lives to make intercession for them." Knowing this should strengthen you each time you start to feel weak. If Jesus is forever praying for you, then you must know that you are a force to be reckoned with. Why? Because Jesus only prays for those who He believes is called to do great things for the kingdom of God. And you, my dear, are one who is called to do great things for the kingdom of God. Do you believe that? Think about it. Look at your life and see what it is saying about who you are in the area of being POWERFUL.

PETITION:

Dear Lord,

You are worthy! Forgive me for not always believing that I am powerful. Thank you for letting me know that I am powerful. Help me to remember each day that I AM POWERFUL.

In Jesus' name, Amen.

D.R.O.P. #5

You Are...

BEAUTIFUL

DEFINITION:

BEAUTIFUL: (*adjective*) having beauty; possessing qualities that give great pleasure or satisfaction to see, hear, think about, etc.; delighting the senses or mind; excellent of its kind.

REFLECTION:

There is a song by Christina Aguilera titled "Beautiful." The hook to the song interchanges from "I" to "You" to "We," stating "You are beautiful, no matter what they say, words can't bring you down. Oh no, you are beautiful, in every single way, yes words can't bring you down. Oh no, so don't you bring me down today." The song speaks of going through things in life that may cause you to feel insecure, ashamed, delirious, empty and so forth. The song continues to state that we are full of beautiful mistakes and that the sun will always shine. The songwriter was getting the point across that no matter what you go through, you must know that you are beautiful, that there is light at the end of the tunnel and that you cannot afford for words to influence you to feel any different.

Would you say that it is challenging to always see the beauty inside and outside of you? There are so many things that can try to alter your perception of yourself as it pertains to beauty. From the experiences that you go through to the comparison of what is beautiful and what is not, to the words that people may have spoken over you, about you, to you, causing you to question yourself all around. Jeremiah 1:5a reads, "Before I formed you in the womb, I knew you." This scripture lets me know that God knows everything about you. Even before your days here on Earth began, He already knew you. He knew what you were going to go through. He knew how you were going to look. He knew what your weaknesses and strengths would be. He knew your future. He knows you!

How wonderful it is to be known, to be understood, to be distinguished. God looks at you and He sees someone that He knows. He is not confusing you with anyone else. He knows that beauty from anywhere. He knows your voice. He knows your name. He knows you. He knew that you would make mistakes and that you would fall short of being perfect. He knew also that you would rise above all situations if you would believe in Him and not give up. He knew that people would challenge your thoughts and that you would fall into the temptation of doubting your worth. And I believe He also knew that one day you would be reading this book and reminded that despite what you have been through and what people may have said, it still doesn't erase the truth that YOU ARE BEAUTIFUL.

OBSERVATION:

Take time to think of how you view yourself. Do you spend time comparing your looks and your life to those around you? Do you find it hard to forgive yourself in certain areas? Do you find yourself complaining? When you look at yourself in the mirror, what do you see? Do you only see your flaws? Do you only see your negative experiences? What you must understand is that there is beauty in every aspect of you. From your mind to your feet, there is something pleasing about you. Do yourself a favor and take time to find the good in the midst of all the bad and thank God for it all. You will find that by being grateful things will turn around for the better and you will begin to feel and be beautiful inside and out. Think about it. Look at your life and see what it is saying about who you are in the area of being BEAUTIFUL.

PETITION:
Dear Lord,

You are great! Forgive me for not always believing that I am beautiful. Thank you for letting me know that I am beautiful. Help me to remember each day that I AM BEAUTIFUL.

In Jesus' name, Amen.

D.R.O.P. #6

You Are...

CREATIVE

DEFINITION:

CREATIVE: (*adjective*) having the quality or power of creating; resulting from originality of thought, expression, etc.; imaginative; originative, productive.

REFLECTION:

One day I was speaking to a close relative of mine and somehow we got into the conversation about being creative and he had said that he didn't have the "creative gene." He had mentioned it was not a part of his make up as a person. My response was that he was creative, but I was not able to give examples at the time because my mind was stuck on the fact that he had already made the vow to himself that the creative gene did not exist inside of him. I asked myself what more can I say to convince him otherwise and the answer I got was nothing. There were no words at the time that would have made him think differently. Any example would have been shot down because his mind was already made up.

The majority of us have heard of the saying, "You are what you think." Matter of fact there is scripture to back up this statement. Proverbs 23:7a reads, "For as he thinks in heart, so is he." So whatever you think about yourself you will become. This is powerful. Another scripture to think about is Matthew 12:34a. It reads, "For out of the abundance of the heart the mouth speaks." Ever wonder what is in your heart? Well, no need to wonder anymore. Just pay attention to the words you have been speaking. Your words will let you know what you think in your heart. From there you can determine who you are. Now, let us go back to being creative.

Being creative comes with every person's make up because we come from a creative God, a God who created everything in seven days! It was actually six days, since He gave himself one day of rest. If we come from a creative God and we were made in His image and His likeness, then what on Earth would make us think that we are not creative?

My thought is comparison. We look around and see what others are doing, how they dress, how they decorate, how they color, how they draw, how they write, how they plan their wedding and then we think to copy what they did since it seems so good compared to what we could do on our own. But the truth is that because you are an original, because you are the only one who can think like you and act like you, then that means you are the only one who can produce a thing in a certain way. It can be something as simple as taking a picture. You know the lighting and the best angle you need. Not everyone knows that, but you do. Why? Because that is your area of expertise and in that area is where YOU ARE CREATIVE.

OBSERVATION:

Take time to think of how you view yourself. Take time to listen to your heart. What have you been speaking lately? What life have you created for yourself through the use of your words? Everything God created in those six days was with a spoken word. And since you are made in His image that means that the life you are living has all been created by the words you have spoken. The words that you speak are from your heart and whatever you think in your heart is who you are. So who are you? And why have you become this person? Does this person best express your creativity? Think about it. Look at your life and see what it is saying about who you are in the area of being CREATIVE.

PETITION:
Dear Lord,

You are righteous! Forgive me for not always believing that I am creative. Thank you for letting me know that I am creative. Help me to remember each day that I AM CREATIVE.

In Jesus' name, Amen.

D.R.O.P. #7

You Are...

UNIQUE

DEFINITION:

UNIQUE: (*adjective*) existing as the only one or as the sole example; single; solitary in type or characteristics; having no like or equal; unparalleled; incomparable.

REFLECTION:

Isn't it amazing to think that every person in the world has different fingerprints? There is not one person who shares the same fingerprints with another. Even identical twins have their own set of fingerprints. And it doesn't just stop at the fingers. It goes to the palm of your hands and to the toes and soles of your feet. How amazing is that?

Many scientists argue over why we have fingerprints. Some say fingerprints are to help with gripping items and others say that is incorrect but they still have no clue as to why they exist or how they are actually formed. To top it all off every person even has their very own bacteria DNA that helps to expose our finger and footprints which becomes very useful to help investigators find the culprit in a criminal matter amongst other things. Once again, how amazing is that!

God is truly amazing. He has purposely created us all to be unequal and in a good way. From the top of your head to the soles of your feet, you are completely original. You are incomparable. You are unparalleled. No one can be you and you can be no one else. You may try to duplicate another person but that will never work out because you were created to be you and your finger and footprints are just reminders of this truth. Your prints are, in my opinion, the stamp of approval that God has given to you to go out in this world and be yourself. He has approved for you to be one of a kind. He has approved for you to be a peculiar person. 1 Peter 2:9 reads, "But you are a chosen generation, a royal priesthood, a holy nation, His own *special people*, that you may proclaim the praises of Him who called you out of darkness into His marvelous light."

You are God's own special person. You are everything that He wanted you to be. He never intended for you to blend in, but rather to stand out. To go out and make a difference wherever your feet lead you. There is no need to complain any longer about why you are not like so-and-so and why you cannot do this-or-that. You have to come to terms with the fact that your identity is found in Christ. And as you spend time with the Lord, you will begin to learn even more things about yourself than you ever knew. You will begin to become confident in who you are. You will begin to accept and appreciate the truth that YOU ARE UNIQUE.

OBSERVATION:

Take time to think of how you view yourself. Point out some things about your personality and your physical appearance and write down what you like and dislike. Then take time to identify how what you like and dislike make you unique or common. Think about how being around certain people make you feel. When you enter into a group setting, familiar and unfamiliar, how do you feel? Does how you feel affect how you act? Are you intimidated to be yourself? Think about it. Look at your life and see what it is saying about who you are in the area of being UNIQUE.

PETITION:

Dear Lord,

You are perfect! Forgive me for not always believing that I am unique. Thank you for letting me know that I am unique. Help me to remember each day that I AM UNIQUE.

In Jesus' name, Amen.

D.R.O.P. #8

You Are...

UNSHAKEABLE

DEFINITIONS:

SHAKE: (*adjective*) to move or sway with short, quick, irregular vibratory movements.; to tremble with emotion, cold, etc., to become dislodged and fall.

UNSHAKEABLE: (*adjective*) unable to be shaken

REFLECTION:

John 10:10 reads, "The thief does not come except to steal, and to kill, and to destroy. I have come that they may have life, and that they may have it more abundantly." In this scripture you will notice two things: The enemy is out to shake you and Jesus came to make you unshakeable.

In life you will find that there are hard times. And hard times can cause you to shift your focus from being happy about life to being mad that life happened. Many times you will hear people say, "I was doing fine, but then life happened." What exactly does that mean? I know when I use the phrase "life happens" I am referring to the fact that sometimes life throws you curveballs including heartache, sickness, betrayal, addiction, abuse, neglect, rejection and death, all of which can sometimes seem unfair or very difficult to get through. You will get through these hard times if you do not surrender to fear and intimidation, but rather surrender to Christ and allow Him to give you the peace of mind that you need to make it through life's moments.

2 Timothy 1:7 reads, "For God has not given us a spirit of fear, but of power and of love and of a sound mind." When life circumstances happen, many times it will try to produce fear. But do not receive that spirit, as this is part of the enemy's plot which is to kill, steal and destroy your life. Once again, the enemy is out to shake you.

Luke 22:31-32 reads, "And the Lord said, "Simon, Simon! Indeed, Satan asked for you, that he may sift you as wheat. But

I have prayed for you, that your faith should not fail; and when you have returned to Me, strengthen your brethren."

Just like Simon, you will go through periods of being sifted. To be sifted means to be separated, to be examined closely, to be scattered. In essence, Satan is examining your life closely. He knows the areas where you are weak and where you are strong. Satan wants to see what you are made of. He wants to separate the strong from the weak. He wants to sift out your strength and only leave you with weakness. The enemy desires to shake you up to see if you really have the faith that you say that you have. He wants to get you all shook up so that you will, in the end, get discouraged and decide to give up and separate yourself from God and the things of God. But take heart! Jesus has prayed for you and is continuously praying that your faith will not fail. And Jesus expects you to make it through the sifting and return back to serving him by way of helping others make it through their sifting moments. And he expects for you to do this because he believes that when you make it through this "life happens" moment, you will come out on top knowing that YOU ARE UNSHAKEABLE.

OBSERVATION:

Take time to think of how you view yourself. Do you see yourself as one who is easily moved by things that take place in your life? Do you find yourself hiding in fear when hardships come your way? Do you find yourself angry about certain things that have taken place in your life causing you to be stagnant in an area? Do you find yourself in a place of weakness and wanting to throw in the towel? Remember that you are stronger than what you may think. You were built to live your life. You have been prepared to play the hand that has been dealt to you. Think about it. Look at your life and see what it is saying about who you are in the area of being UNSHAKEABLE.

PETITION:
Dear Lord,

You are lovely! Forgive me for not always believing that I am unshakeable. Thank you for letting me know that I am unshakeable. Each day, help me to remember that I AM UNSHAKEABLE.

In Jesus' name, Amen.

D.R.O.P. #9

You Are...

MEMORABLE

DEFINITION:

MEMORABLE: (*adjective*) worth remembering; notable; easily remembered.

REFLECTION:

There was a time in my life where I was bombarded with thoughts of being replaceable. I was being attacked once again in my mind about whether life would be better off without me in it. This is an attack the enemy had out on me since I was a teenager that followed me to my adulthood. Although it was not a consistent thought, it was a recurring one that would show up every now and again. I remember one time the thought showed up while I was sitting at my desk writing notes. It startled me because I really did not know from what angle that thought crept in, but I knew that I had to fight it by replacing that thought with one that promoted my life. When the "you are replaceable" thought came in, I remember I did not fight it instantly. I allowed the thought to soak in causing me to feel like life would be best without me in it. I kept thinking I was replaceable in my marriage, my job and my ministry. Later, after I had decided to combat that thought, it dawned on me, "I may be replaceable but I am about to be missed." I thought this and began to say it to myself with such confidence.

What I was saying to myself was that if I was replaceable, then at the very least you are going to remember me. You are going to remember me because whatever I do, I do as unto the Lord. And doing things as unto the Lord means that you give your best. And people will always remember someone who gave their best while they were alive. The Bible says in Colossians 3:23-24, "And whatever you do, do it heartily, as to the Lord and not to men, knowing that from the Lord you will receive the reward of the inheritance; for you serve the Lord Christ."

Many times we fail to give our best in life because we fail to remember why we are supposed to do what it is that we do.

From loving someone, to working our job, to helping others, we are supposed to do it all as if we were serving the Lord. Why? Because if we do things for people while not remembering Christ, we will find ourselves doing things half-heartedly and based on our feelings. Our feelings tell us that because our spouse is rude to us, we don't have to be kind toward them. Our feelings tell us that because our boss is a hot mess, we don't have to perform at our highest level. Our feelings tell us that because that person cut us off while driving, we too can speed up and cut them off. Our feelings make us unbalanced and emotional causing us to never be consistent in doing things the right way because our feelings constantly fluctuate based on the day and how things are going and even more importantly, how we are thinking. This is why we have to do things as unto the Lord because when you think about serving the Lord you think about giving Him your best because He deserves it.

God wants to see you at your best. And your best is only achieved when you involve Christ in it. No matter what the circumstance may be, you must remember to consult God and get the wisdom of the Holy Spirit on how to do your best in every area of your life. And this does not mean that you have to do things perfectly all the time because sometimes your feelings will "get the best of you." But in the end, know that you are in charge of your feelings and you can tell them what to do. Remind yourself that you will do things as unto the Lord because you desire to live your best life. And living your best life will, in the end, cause you to be celebrated. Because when you give your best, you leave an impression. At your best, you will find that you are impressive. You are noteworthy. YOU ARE MEMORABLE.

OBSERVATION:

Take time to think of how you view yourself. Do you see yourself as one who is worth being remembered? (Side Note: the answer should be yes! You are so important! Please know that.) When you think of all the time and energy you put into things, would you say that you will leave an impression? Do you find yourself living to please men versus living to please God? Can you say that you are living your best life? Think about it. Look at your life and see what it is saying about who you are in the area of being MEMORABLE.

PETITION:

Dear Lord,

You are constant! Forgive me for not always believing that I am memorable. Thank you for letting me know that I am memorable. Help me to remember each day that I AM MEMORABLE.

In Jesus' name, Amen.

D.R.O.P. #10

You Are...

COURAGEOUS

DEFINITIONS:

COURAGE: (*noun*) the quality of mind or spirit that enables a person to face difficulty, danger, pain, etc.; without fear; bravery.

COURAGEOUS: (*adjective*) possessing or characterized by courage; brave.

REFLECTION:

When I think about being courageous I think about being bold. And when you are bold, you say what needs to be said and do what needs to be done without the anchor of fear holding you back. Yes, sometimes you may do and say what is necessary with some timidity, but in the end you choose to press through the fear and reach your point of destiny. Destiny is another word for future.

Future is defined as something that will exist or happen in the time to come. Your future is based on your ability to continue to walk this life out one day at a time. And in each day you will have many moments, many opportunities to make every minute, every second, count. We have all been allotted the same amount of time in a day. It is up to each of us to decide how we will use that time to help make our future brighter. You have the ability to help steer your future to your appointed destiny. You can also think of destiny as a destination.

Destination is defined as the place to which a person or thing travels or is sent. Each of us have been created to "go somewhere in life." This is a phrase that you may have said to yourself or heard others say when referring to someone and how their life is appearing. Many times if someone is not making good choices an outside person may comment, "She is not going anywhere in life. She's just making bad choices, doing her own thing and not caring anymore." In this instance, we have a final say of someone's life based on what they are currently portraying, because what you exhibit in your life leads to the prediction of how your life will turn out. Will you go somewhere or will you stay in the same place? Will you move forward with your life or will stay repeating a cycle in life?

A cycle will have you think that you are going somewhere only to find that you end up right back in the same place. Over and over again, you think you have left your past and as you move forward, you find that you actually have been moving backwards except this time it may be with a different person or in a different location. Your mindset is an illusion. You have been deceived, thinking that you were going somewhere but in reality you were headed back to a place of being stuck. And when you are stuck you cannot move unless you get help to get you out. In this case, the help that you need to get you pulled out of the same muddy pit is the help of Jesus Christ.

Deuteronomy 31:6 reads, "Be strong and of good courage, do not fear nor be afraid of *them*; for the Lord your God, he is the one who goes with you. He will not leave you nor forsake you." In this particular scripture, Moses was sharing with the people of Israel what God spoke to him regarding taking over nations and not being afraid of them. In your particular situation, who or what is your "them" that the Lord may be telling you not to fear? Is your "them" family members, peers, a significant other, your boss, writing, driving, flying, addiction or public speaking? Whatever it may be, God is instructing you to not be discouraged and to not be in fear because he is with you. He will help you get through it all so that you can reach your destiny. He has a planned future for you and he promises that he will be there with you every step of the way.

You do not have to stay in the same cycle of life thinking that you are moving forward only to find that you have returned to the place from which you started. You are able to move forward and end up in your destined place in life if you walk out in faith and do and say what you believe God is instructing you to do and say. Your destination in life awaits you. You do not have to give others the power to have the final say in your life. Sure right now you may be lost and not certain which road to take but if you just trust and believe God He will direct your path. Even if you have to do it afraid just take that first step knowing that God is with you. And as you continue to take more steps, you will find that fear will be left behind and faith will continue to be right alongside of you helping you keep your eyes on the prize which is your future. Do not be discouraged. Do not be dismayed. You can walk this life out and reach your destination. Even with all the detours, if you follow God's leading you will end up where you were meant to go. You can do this. You can walk this thing out. You can make it. How do I know this? Because YOU ARE COURAGEOUS.

OBSERVATION:

Take time to think of how you view yourself. Do you find yourself repeating the same cycle in life? Do you find yourself wanting more but staying with lack? Do you find that your actions and your speech are going two different directions? When it comes to moving toward your destination, you have to make sure that what you are saying is lining up with what you are doing and vice versa. I am reminded of the story of the tower of Babel (Hebrews 11). The people were able to build as their speech was the same. But the moment that God changed their speech and caused all of them to have different languages, they were no longer able to build together to reach their destination. The same will apply to you. If your actions and words are not aligned, then you will not be able to go where you were meant to go. Faith and courage will have to outweigh fear every time. This will be the only way you can move forward toward your appointed future. Think about it. Look at your life and see what it is saying about who you are in the area of being COURAGEOUS.

PETITION:

Dear Lord,

You are mighty! Forgive me for not always believing that I am courageous. Thank you for letting me know that I am courageous. Help me to remember each day that I AM COURAGEOUS.

In Jesus' name, Amen.

D.R.O.P. #11

You Are...

UNDERSTANDING

DEFINITION:

UNDERSTANDING: (*noun*) mental process of a person who comprehends; comprehension; personal interpretation; intelligence; superior power of discernment; enlightened intelligence.

REFLECTION:

If you ask a group of people what they desire most from someone, then they most likely will say, "Respect." There is something about being respected that makes a difference with how we get along with others. The moment that we become or feel disrespected, we then either get upset, offended or separate ourselves from those who disrespected us. From cutting us off on the road, to cussing us out on the streets, spreading a rumor, not returning our phone call or forgetting our birthday, you name it, there will always be reason to feel disrespected. And sometimes it is not even intentional.

Aretha Franklin said it best in her song, "Respect." At the end of her song she sings, "R-E-S-P-E-C-T find out what it means to me." This is very important in dealing with relationships. We have to know what respect means to that person to ensure that we do our best not to disrespect them especially if it is a relationship that we desire to keep. Knowing what respect means to another person will also help us not judge them so easily.

Many times when we do not know what respect means to others, we will find ourselves judging them for their responses to our behavior. This is because we do not fully know them or how they think. We lack an understanding because we have not spent enough time with them to get to know their likes and dislikes, their past mistakes and future goals. We lack getting to know who they truly are. And in order to know who someone really is, it will require much time and attention.

Your time is just about the most important possession in your life next to money. Have you ever heard the saying, "Time is money?" Well, I believe it is true. Because what you do with your time will cost you something. It will cost you missing out on something else in exchange for what you are giving your time to in that moment. What you do with your time will determine what your priorities are in life. Your attention goes side by side with time because what you spend time doing automatically requires your attention. And attention costs as well. You hear it all the time, I am sure, especially if you have children you may say it all the time. "Pay attention."

To pay for something means to give money in exchange for an item. So when you pay attention, you are in essence giving your time in exchange for an understanding of what to do. Being attentive means that you give over your five senses to what is being done and or said. In the end you will reap the harvest of comprehending from the time that you had sown into paying attention.

The Bible reads in Proverbs 4:7, "Wisdom is the principal thing; therefore get wisdom. And in all your getting, get understanding." This verse lets me know that as important as it may be to have wisdom in your life, what you really need in addition, is an understanding. You need to know why situations occur, why people act the way that they do and why you act the way that you do. You need to have an understanding because, in my opinion, that is the only way that you will be able to walk in love with yourself and others which is what Christ really desires for us to do. But how can you love someone when you do not understand them? How can you forgive someone for their actions when you do not know what was the force behind their actions? How can you live peaceably with others when you do not know how to wisely deal with them? Yes, understanding is of importance, and it will take much of your time and energy which, for many, will feel like it is not worth it. And being worth your time means that you see the value in doing what is being presented.

I want to propose getting to know those around you so that you will be able to truly walk in love with them. Take time to find out what it means to respect your friends, your spouse, your family members and your neighbors. Take time to get to know why those around you make the choices they make. Take time to gain wisdom so that you can know what choices to make and who to love up close or from a distance. Take time to get to know yourself so that you can then pass on that love to others by getting to know them. Yes, I know it will cost you time, attention and energy, but in the end you will find that it was worth it. Your time spent getting to know and respect yourself and others will be worth it because you will get a return receipt stating that YOU ARE UNDERSTANDING.

OBSERVATION:

Take time to think of how you view yourself. Do you find that it is important to get to know others? Do you take time to get to know yourself? Do you ever wonder why you behave the way that you do? Your time is so valuable you must have wisdom to know how to spend it. Who or what is taking up most of your time throughout your days? Is that person, place or thing worth it? It is important that you begin to find a healthy balance in your life by writing down a list of your priorities. Once you know what your priorities are, then you will be able to know how to spend your time. Spending time getting to know yourself and others is of importance, but where it falls on your list of priorities is up to you. Think about it. Look at your life and see what it is saying about who you are in the area of being UNDERSTANDING.

PETITION:

Dear Lord,

You are all-knowing! Forgive me for not always believing that I am understanding. Thank you for letting me know that I am understanding. Help me to remember each day that I AM UNDERSTANDING.

In Jesus' name, Amen.

D.R.O.P. #12

You Are...

BLESSED

DEFINITION:

BLESSED: (*adjective*) divinely or supremely favored; fortunate; blissfully happy or contented; bringing happiness and thankfulness

REFLECTION:

In life there are many highs and many lows. There are times when you feel like everything is working out in your favor and times when you feel like things are not working out as you had hoped. During these times, you may fluctuate from feeling blessed to feeling cursed. Like a teeter-totter, you go up and down giving full way to each side every time you are moved.

It's like you have life on one side and death on the other side, both taking turns and all the while you may feel like you have no control. But the truth is that you do have control. And the control that you have is in what you choose to believe.

The other day I was reading the book of Luke and I ran across this scripture which really enlightened me. In Luke 1:45 it reads, "You are blessed because you believed that the Lord would do what he said." (This was what Elizabeth said to Mary while pregnant with Jesus.) Once I read that scripture, I thought, "wow." It was said so simply, but had such a profound impact as I meditated on that word.

As I kept repeating the verse I realized we are blessed the moment that we believe what God says. You may not have what you believe in your physical hands yet, but the moment that you prayed for what you believed was the moment that you became blessed. What this says to me is that you do not have to wait for something to manifest in your life before you can begin to be blissfully happy, as the definition suggests. Nope. You do not have to wait to get what you desire before you can begin to be thankful. You are blessed from the moment you believe! A blessed person will exhibit they are blessed by their inward feeling of thankfulness and outward expression of happiness beyond measure.

Blessed people are those who cannot be moved from what they believe God said that he would do. Blessed people are those who see what is going on around them and still believe that God will bring them through. Blessed people are those who trust that all things will work out for their good. Blessed people are those who know that they are divinely favored by God. Blessed people are those who know that regardless of where they come from, their expected end is prosperous. Blessed people are those who call things that be not as though they were. Blessed people are those who are able to wait on the Lord and gain strength in the process. Blessed people are those who know that God is not through with them yet. Blessed people are those who are able to count it all joy when they go through diverse test and trials. Blessed people are those who stand on God's word!

So even if you do not have the physical manifestation of a fancy car, dope house, highest position in your company, spouse of your dreams, complete healing in your body, non-profit/for profit business, whatever it is that you are in belief of, the truth is that you are not cursed but rather YOU ARE BLESSED because you believe!

OBSERVATION:

Take time to think of how you view yourself. Do you view yourself as one who is highly favored or do you view yourself as one who is damned? Do you think that because you have been in the same poverty position for years that you will always remain there? Do you see others around you happy and think to yourself that you would be happy too if you had what you wanted? Do you believe the lies of the enemy over the truth of God's word? It is time to check your list of what you are in belief of to receive and begin to thank God for it in advance. It is time to shut your mouth from saying negative things that will waver your belief. I am reminded of this text in the Bible where Zechariah's prayer for a son was being answered but then he began to question how God would be able to do it, being that he was at an old age. As a result, the angel, Gabriel, had to shut Zechariah's mouth until the child was born so Zechariah would not forfeit his blessing (Luke 1:19-20). Are you forfeiting your right to be blessed? Think about it. Look at your life and see what it is saying about who you are in the area of being BLESSED.

PETITION:

Dear Lord,

You are ever present! Forgive me for not always believing that I am blessed. Thank you for letting me know that I am blessed. Help me to remember each day that I AM BLESSED.

In Jesus' name, Amen.

D.R.O.P. #13

You Are...

QUALIFIED

DEFINITION:

QUALIFIED: (*adjective*) having the qualities, accomplishments, etc., that fit a person for some function, office, or the like; modified, limited, or restricted in some way.

REFLECTION:

When I was a young girl (around the second grade) my mom had decided to have me and my siblings join our city track team, the Oxnard Stars. It was there that I learned what it meant to be a disciplined athlete. We would have to go to practice just about every weekday in order to be fully prepared for our track meets that took place on the weekends. Track meets were where we would meet other track teams to compete. We trained all week in order to be conditioned and ready to do our best on the day of competition.

It was during our practices and at our track meets that our coaches (and the athletes for that matter) could really identify what event was the right one for us. For example, my coach and I realized that I was not necessarily a sprinter but rather a long-distance runner. In sprints I did well, but not as good as I did in long distance. It was as if the longer I ran, the faster I became; but the shorter I ran, the slower I felt (in comparison to all the other fast athletes). I still did the 4x100 and 4x400 all the way through my high school years but that was the extent of my sprints. Other than that, I was a long-distance runner all day and, for the most part, I loved it.

When it came to the start of each race we had an official who had a fake gun. He would say those infamous words, "On your mark. Get set. Go!" And at the sound of "Go!" there would simultaneously be a gun shot in the air to make it all the more exciting. The only time it was not exciting for a runner, yet suspenseful for the audience, was when you would hear the gun go off multiple times signifying that someone had "jumped the gun." This meant that before the gun was shot, a runner had already left their mark and started to run, which would eventually cause a disqualification, and you could no longer compete in that particular event for that day, but you could try to compete again at the following track meet. You would get a second chance at a later time.

Looking at it now, this reminds me of what can happen to us in life today. Many of us may have been practicing for something all of our lives or for months and years on end perfecting our craft in order to become the best singer, actor, business owner, minister, hair stylist, fashion designer, food inspector, athlete, etc., all of which we would say we were qualified to become since we have put in so much time and effort in that area. But the problem is when we move too soon, when we "jump the gun" and move from our current position before God says, "Go!"

When we move from one place to another without the consultation of the Holy Spirit and God's approval, then many times we will find ourselves frustrated with the process and disappointed with the outcome. I am reminded of the book of Ruth. Ruth had to wait for her mother-in-law, Naomi, to give her the go-ahead on when to make a bold move toward Boaz. Naomi told Ruth that Boaz would then tell Ruth what to do. Ruth was instructed by Naomi to listen to Boaz and do as he says. Ruth took the instructions of Naomi and in the end she received what she desired which was to marry Boaz and redeem her family lineage by giving birth to a son. Imagine if Ruth had not listened to Naomi's instructions and decided to do things her way and at her pace. Perhaps then she would have messed up the opportunity that was presented before her. Perhaps then she would have never become Mrs. Boaz and her future of having a legacy would have been tarnished.

This is why it is important to know the timing of God for your life. It is important to be able to know when it is time for you to elevate to your next place in life. Continue to practice your talent and prepare to be put into a place of authority in that area but wait to make that big move until after you hear God's voice of approval. You do not want to be disqualified by moving too soon. Sure you may get another chance in that area but it will have to be at a later time and perhaps with a different setting or person. So in the meantime do not only work at perfecting your gift but also work on your attitude and your character. There's a saying, "Your gifting will take you where your character cannot keep you." You do not want that to be your story. Yes, you are able. Yes, you are capable. Yes, you are fitted. But be sure not to move until you hear the words, "On your mark. Get set. Go!" It is your time to shine! YOU ARE QUALIFIED.

OBSERVATION:

Take time to think of how you view yourself. If the opportunity presented itself for you to do what you have always wanted to do, then would you say that you are prepared? Have you taken time to seek God's face to know what your purpose in life may be? Have you taken time to know yourself to find out what you are talented in doing? Do you find yourself moving from place to place in jobs, relationships or residential areas? Are you working on your attitude/character so that you can be the best you in the area of your expertise? Think about it. Look at your life and see what it is saying about who you are in the area of being QUALIFIED.

PETITION:

Dear Lord,

You are able! Forgive me for not always believing that I am qualified. Thank you for letting me know that I am qualified. Help me to remember each day that I AM QUALIFIED.

In Jesus' name, Amen.

D.R.O.P. #14

You Are...

JUSTIFIED

DEFINITION:

JUSTIFIED: (*verb-used with an object*) to show (an act, claim, statement, etc.) to be just or right; to defend or uphold as warranted or well-grounded; theology to declare innocent or guiltless; absolve; acquit of much or great significance or consequence.

REFLECTION:

In my life, I have met a lot of people who have a victim mentality, a "woe is me" mindset. A mindset that if anyone does anything to them, they become a victim and as a result have self-pity and want others to see them as being mistreated. While they very well could have been mistreated, staying in that mindset will hinder their future. I am not judging them because I, too, understand what it is like to live in a place of self-pity thinking that no one understands me but me. Funny and great thing is that I cannot fully give examples of being there because I have been far removed from that mindset. Praise God! Still, I do remember that I once was that person, but more than that I was once that person who felt so ashamed about the lifestyle that I had chosen and the deeds that I had done which were hard to break free from mentally.

In my mind, I knew the actions that I had done that brought shame to my name. I remember a time where I did not like my name Emerald. I felt like I made a fool of that name because I gave myself to some guy who I had defiled myself with time and time again. I did inappropriate acts as a single woman who believed in Christ and I was okay with it at the time, but once I had fully come to know Christ, I was ashamed and completely disappointed in myself. Philippians 3:7 reads, "But whatever were gains to me I now consider loss for the sake of Christ." In this verse, Paul was speaking about being one who had reason to boast but now that he had come to know Christ he had realized that what he was once proud of was something he no longer was proud of. His past was now something he needed to repent, and that is where I found myself. Have you ever found yourself in need of repentance?

What I have learned is that there is nothing too hard for God, even in the place of forgiveness. He is able and willing to forgive you of your past, present and future, wrongful deeds and bring you to a place of repentance where you will make a choice to turn from your selfish ways and begin to live for him. Philippians 3:19 says, "Their destiny is destruction, their god is their stomach, and their glory is in their shame. Their mind is set on earthly things." We must be careful not to fall under this description. Our glory cannot be in the shameful things that we do. Our minds cannot be set on earthly things but on the truth that we are citizens of Heaven, therefore we have to be representatives of Christ at all times.

Sure you may have made mistakes in your past, but you are no longer bound to those mistakes if you have repented and turned from those ways. Things that you may have done such as murder, adultery, sexual immorality, drunkenness and the like, all of those things have been washed away by the blood of Christ. Yes, you may have been convicted of those acts and you should have served a deep punishment for it all, but by the grace of God you did not have to pay that price. God saw fit to allow Jesus to plead for your case to prove that you are innocent because of Christ's willingness to die for your sins. What a glorious thing it is to know that Christ stood in the gap for you and continually does, believing in the greatness inside of you and denying the sins of your past the power to destroy your future. You no longer have to feel ashamed. You no longer have to be a victim to what you have experienced in your past. You no longer have to rehearse the wrongful deeds done toward you by others or by yourself. You no longer have to live in a place of condemnation. You no longer have to be defined by your sins. Why? Because of the goodness of Christ who is on your side and declares that YOU ARE JUSTIFIED.

OBSERVATION:

Take time to think of how you view yourself. Knowing that you have not always lived a pure lifestyle, do you still see yourself as dirty or guilty? Do you still find yourself doing those things that you know in the end will bring shame to Christ's name? Have you ever considered harming yourself because you felt like what you did is too much for God to forgive? I am reminded of Peter and Judas. Both disciples had denied Christ and betrayed Him in their own way. Peter was able to muster up the courage to ask Christ for forgiveness and he was forgiven. But Judas felt like his deed of betraying Christ was too big to be forgiven even worse he must have felt like he could never forgive himself. So due to condemnation Judas hung himself. If only he knew that Christ was going to come back to life three days after his crucifixion. Perhaps then he would not have beat himself up so much or felt like he was better off dead. Perhaps if he had repented he would have been told by God that he would get the chance to see Christ again and ask for forgiveness. But that chance was taken by his choice to kill himself for the wrong he had done. Please do not harm yourself or commit suicide because of the sin you have done or because of the sins that been done toward you. Know that Christ will plead on your behalf. Sure you may have to walk out the cost of that sin by way of jail, prison, ended relationships, etc., but you still have a purpose to fulfill. You still have others to help in the area where you were once bound. Think about it. Look at your life and see what it is saying about who you are in the area of being JUSTIFIED.

PETITION:
Dear Lord,

You are just! Forgive me for not always believing that I am justified. Thank you for letting me know that I am justified. Help me to remember each day that I AM JUSTIFIED.

In Jesus' name, Amen.

D.R.O.P. #15

You Are...

RESILIENT

DEFINITION:

RESILIENT: (*adjective*) Springing back; rebounding; returning to the original form or position after being bent, compressed or stretched; recovering from illness, depression, adversity, or the like; buoyant.

REFLECTION:

When I was a young girl, there was this one toy that many children had to have called a slinky. A slinky is described as a pre-compressed helical spring toy that is able to perform numerous tricks like traveling down a flight of steps end-over-end as it stretches and reforms itself with the aid of gravity and its own momentum. What I loved about playing with a slinky

71

was that you could twist and turn it and it would always go back to its same slinky state.

There were times when we would get the slinky and partner up to pull it apart as far as we could. One person would then let go of their side of the slinky while the other kept a grip on their end. We would eagerly wait to see the slinky bounce right back into place with force. We also tried to really wrangle it, which in those cases, we would sometimes bend the springs a little too much where it would spring back together but just not as in tack due to the now severely mangled springs. But still, it was able to be identified as a slinky just with some need of detangling. Can anyone relate?

Many of us today are much like this slinky. We have been through ups and downs, twists and turns, overs and unders, ins and outs, only to find ourselves bouncing back to a place of determination. When you go through tests, trials and tribulations, it is going to take determination to get you back to where you desire to be. Like a slinky, you will need the aid of gravity (the soundness of the Holy Spirit) and your own momentum (self-will and determination) to get you back to your original state after going through your circumstances. It is not God's intention for you to go through life alone. It is not God's intention for you to give up. It is not God's intention for you to feel forsaken. God's intention for you is to press through your situation and live to say that you made it! And not only did you make it, but you are thriving in life as a result of your trust in Him.

Isaiah 40:31 reads, "But those who trust in the Lord will find new strength. They will soar high on wings like eagles. They will run and not grow weary. They will walk and not faint."

As a believer in Christ, your strength to continue to move forward and not grow weary or faint is based on your ability to trust in the Lord. You must trust that He has plans for you to prosper and not to harm you. You must trust that he will not forsake you. You must trust that he will take your cares away. You must trust that he has given you the Holy Spirit to help guide, comfort, counsel and befriend you. You must trust that his son, Jesus Christ, is forever interceding for you. Meaning that Jesus is forever praying on your behalf believing and knowing that you will pass the test, you will make it through your situation. You must trust that you are like a slinky, always able to bounce back into your original healthy state. You must trust that God's word is true. You must trust and believe that YOU ARE RESILIENT.

OBSERVATION:

Take time to think of how you view yourself. Do you see yourself as one who is determined? Do you find yourself wishing that things would change but unwilling to do anything to make things better? Do you find yourself living in a place of procrastination and silence? Do you desire to get back to where you once were in life? Sometimes we can stay in a place of wishing and hoping for better but not making an effort to do anything about our situation. Many times this could be due to an overwhelming feeling of doubt that things will get better for you. In these times, it is best not to isolate yourself but to reach out to others for help so that you will not drown in your worry and discouragement. You are worth pressing forward. Philippians 3:13-14 reads, "No, dear brothers and sisters, I have not achieved it, but I focus on this one thing: Forgetting the past and looking forward to what lies ahead, I press on to reach the end of the race and receive the heavenly prize for which God, through Christ Jesus, is calling us." God is calling you to run your race. You stop for help when needed. Take a water break, stretch, condition, do what you have to do to get you back in the race of life. No need to look back but focus on what is in front of you. The ribbon at the finish line is all yours for the taking. Will you continue to run your race? Think about it. Look at your life and see what it is saying about who you are in the area of being RESILIENT.

PETITION:

Dear Lord,

You are honored! Forgive me for not always believing that I am resilient. Thank you for letting me know that I am resilient. Help me to remember each day that I AM RESILIENT.

In Jesus' name, Amen.

D.R.O.P. #16

You Are...

SMART

DEFINITION:

SMART: (*adjective*) quick or prompt in action, as persons.; having or showing quick intelligence or ready mental capability; dashingly or impressively neat or trim in appearance, as persons, dress, etc.; socially elegant; sophisticated or fashionable; saucy.

REFLECTION:

I remember when I was in the fourth grade. I practically had begged my mom to buy me glasses so that I could wear them at school. For some reason I would see my classmates who wore glasses and thought that they looked smart. They looked like they were studious. They looked like they knew more than I did and it was all because they wore glasses. So eventually my mom took me to the optometrist and the conclusion was that I did not need to wear glasses. That should have been great news but it wasn't for me. I wanted glasses! Somehow, my mom managed to buy me some rose-pink framed glasses with no prescription and I was able to wear them at school. I do not recall how long I wore them but I do remember having them and having a sense of accomplishment by just having them on my face.

Fast forward to my college years and again this urge for glasses hit me. I so badly wanted to wear glasses but still did not need them as my eyesight was perfect. It was not until I graduated from graduate school that my brother had given me the gift of purple framed glasses with no prescription and I absolutely loved them! I wore those rectangle shaped frames and felt like I looked super smart and cute I may add. Eventually one side of the glasses broke and I had to throw them away, but I loved having them while they were in my possession.

Thinking back, I remember that when I would wear my purple framed glasses my eyes would eventually start to bother me. I think it was the fact that I was looking through a lens that I did not need and that additional layer affected my sight. This is a perfect example of why we need to be honest with ourselves and be okay with what the truth is so that we can be the best us that we can be. In my case, I did not need glasses. I should have been okay with that truth and focus on not just looking smart, but actually being smart. It is not enough to look a part, but important to be that part as well.

Many times we tend to focus more on our outward appearance than our inward assurance. Imagine if we took the necessary time to study our fields of interests, learn more about our communities, listen to the news to see what we need to pray about, focused on building our character so that we could be prepared for the next level that God plans to take us. Imagine that. Wouldn't that be smart of us to do? And what I have learned is that when we focus on being our best selves inward, then that is when our outward appearance follows suit. It goes hand and hand. Working on your inside (mind, emotions, will, imagination, intellect—your soul) will be followed by a better looking you.

So if you are up for the challenge of being smart in the sense of getting to know who you are in order to see what needs to be worked on, then now is the time to begin to study to show yourself approved. In 2 Timothy 2:15 it reads, "Work hard so you can present yourself to God and receive his approval. Be a good worker, one who does not need to be ashamed and who correctly explains the word of truth." I believe that this can be applied to the area of being smart. It takes work to get to know who you are and to not be ashamed about where you have come from or how you may be different in comparison to others. It takes work to study and be able to build up your intelligence to become an expert in your field of interest. It takes work to be able to learn your community and know how to handle things correctly. It takes work to be the best you and to then have the confidence to present your best self to God for his approval (yes, God loves you as you are, but he still wants to see the greatness inside of you come out for others to benefit from). It takes work but it is worth the time and effort. It is your time to use your time wisely to not only look impressive but to be impressive. You have the capability. So go ahead and invest in yourself. I know you will do it because YOU ARE SMART.

OBSERVATION:

Take time to think of how you view yourself. What type of smart are you? According to the definition, there are different levels of being smart. There are fashion, intelligence, social sophistication, and being a "smart aleck." Then there are other types of smart that we hear such as "book smart" and "street smart." What I have learned is that we all have a level of smartness, we just need to identify which one it is so that we can improve on the other types of being smart. But with being smart, we also need to be wise so that we can apply our intellect in the right way. Moving on to our outward appearance, what is it about the need for some of us to look smart? Could it be true that the way you dress can affect the way that you feel? Could it be true that just by taking care of yourself by showering, dressing nice and accessorizing with glasses that we begin to sound intelligent or even thrive to be intelligent? Or is it true that if you take time to be a better you on the inside, looking good will naturally follow? I wonder. Think about it. Look at your life and see what it is saying about who you are in the area of being SMART.

PETITION:
Dear Lord,

You are Magnificent! Forgive me for not always believing that I am smart. Thank you for letting me know that I am smart. Help me to remember each day that I AM SMART.

In Jesus' name, Amen.

D.R.O.P. #17

You Are...

CURRENT

DEFINITION:

CURRENT: (*adjective*) passing in time; belonging to the time actually passing; prevalent; customary; popular.

REFLECTION:

For many years, I lived in a place of insecurity. I was insecure about my outward appearance, about how I spoke, about what I possessed. The list goes on and on. But one day (I don't know exactly when but I know it was a long process), I woke up and no longer found myself being insecure as I once had been. I no longer found myself jealous of others but rather embracing them and myself. I had learned that by me accepting those I was jealous of; I was then able to accept myself. There was no need to compare myself anymore. There was no need to put someone else down to make me feel good. There was no need to put myself down to esteem someone else. Nope. There was no need for any of that in my life. That chapter had come to a close. And the new mindset that came to me was that "I am always in."

"I am always in" means that I am always accepted, I am always welcomed, I am always necessary for this life. I am not old news. I am relevant. Whether others think this to be true or not, the most important thing is that I believe it to be true. So I chose to accept myself, to welcome myself, to believe that I am needed for this life that I have been given. Others need me and I need others so that we can become the best us that we can be. I cannot pretend to know everything. There are some things that I am not aware of or have not studied much about that another person is astute in and qualified to share what they know with me so that I can now be alert in that area as well. We don't have to pretend to know it all. We do have to be truthful and identify our areas of weakness so that we can be made strong by those around us. This is all part of God's plan.

Proverbs 27:17 reads, "As iron sharpens iron, so a friend sharpens a friend." This scripture lets me know that we need one another to be the best us. We need to have at least one good friend who will be honest with us at all times so that we can become sharp in areas where we have found ourselves dull. And that one good friend needs you for the same reason. You are what someone needs to stay in tune with themselves and to hold themselves accountable to the areas of which they are trying not to stumble in and vice versa. But we have to be willing to be vulnerable and accountable all at the same time.

You have to be vulnerable enough to admit that you have fallen short and accountable enough to take responsibility for your actions. It must be understood that falling short or "missing the mark" does not equate to you no longer being "always in." No. The truth is that you are still accepted. You are still welcomed. You are still necessary for this life. Your shortcomings do not eradicate your importance. It does not give permission for you to now be counted out. You are still a vital part to the body of Christ.

Ephesians 4:16 says, "He makes the whole body fit together perfectly. As each part does its own special work, it helps the other parts grow, so that the whole body is healthy and growing and full of love."

You are a necessary part to help keep the body of Christ healthy. You fit perfectly. There is no need for you to live in a place of insecurity questioning who you are or how you look. You are God's child and you look the way he has designed for you to look. Can you improve and be a better you inside and out? Sure you can, and you are encouraged to do so. But as long as you know that you cannot do it without the help of God and those who He has placed around you for a purpose. You are accepted. You are welcomed. You are necessary. YOU ARE CURRENT.

OBSERVATION:

Take time to think of how you view yourself. Do you see yourself as necessary for others to draw from? Do you see yourself as one who has answers to current day problems? Do you believe that you were created for such a time as this? When you look at yourself in the mirror, do you see someone who is tired and worn out or someone who is refreshed and ready for their next promotion? Take time out to reflect on your present thoughts of yourself. Remind yourself that you are a needed part to the body of Christ. Ask God to reveal to you what part you play to help make this world a better place. Think about it. Look at your life and see what it is saying about who you are in the area of being CURRENT.

PETITION:

Dear Lord,

You are True! Forgive me for not always believing that I am current. Thank you for letting me know that I am current. Help me to remember each day that I AM CURRENT.

In Jesus' name, Amen.

D.R.O.P. #18

You Are...

REDEEMED

DEFINITION:

REDEEM: (*verb*) to buy or pay off; clear by payment; to exchange for money or goods; to make up for; make amends for; offset (some fault, shortcoming, etc.); Theology. To deliver from sin and its consequences by means of a sacrifice offered for the sinner.

REFLECTION:

The other day I was watching this show on Hulu titled "The Next Kids Food Network Star." In this episode, the kids had to taste a mystery ingredient in front of the camera and explain how it tastes and how you could use it in a dish. Some of the kids who made mistakes and did not do their best said out loud to themselves, "I have to redeem myself." Each kid was going to get another opportunity to prove they have what it takes to be the first Kids Food Network Star in the next challenge. When I heard them say, "I have to redeem myself," I could not help but wonder if they really knew what the word "redeem" meant. They are young and smart in their area of expertise but do they really know what it means to be redeemed?

Ephesian 1:7 reads, "He is so rich in kindness and grace that he purchased our freedom with the blood of his Son and forgave our sins." Going back to the definition of redeem, you will find that in this scripture, we have been redeemed by God sacrificing his son, Jesus Christ, to die for our sins. God purchased our freedom by the captivity of Christ who then died on our behalf and rose again to life once again on our behalf. Jesus then leaves the Holy Spirit to dwell within us while here on Earth so that we can be guided to choose life and not death, blessings and not curses, right and not wrong, so that we will have the power to resist temptation and not sin. And God did all of this because he loves us. His kindness and grace is like no other. Jesus was exchanged for the goods; which is us. We are the goods.

Goods is defined as possessions, especially movable effects or personal property; merchandise. In addition to Jesus Christ, we are God's most precious possessions. We are God's merchandise. God has purchased us at the high cost of his one and only son. He believed that we were worth every penny that was used for betrayal, every stone that was thrown, every lash that was given, every assaultive word that was spoken, every spit that was spewed, we were worth Christ's crucifixion. Wow. God believed that we were worth the investment.

Within us is the ability to multiply. Within us is the ability to take our talents, perfect them and share them with the world with the goal of receiving resources as well as influencing others to accept the offer to become God's goods. We have not been purchased to sit on the shelf and collect dust, but to be used for God's kingdom and produce. When you think about a person being purchased, you may instantly think of slavery, but that is not the viewpoint nor is it the truth of why God purchased us. We were not purchased to be exploited. Rather we were purchased to be loved. Consider being purchased as adoption.

There are millions of children who are considered orphans and only thousands who get adopted. Being one who has worked in the group home sector for over a decade I can say that from my experience, many families do not want to adopt children specifically who are 16 years and older and have a bad history.

But unlike us, God does not care about your history. So even if you have a history of AWOLing, fighting, abuse, emotional disturbance, and so forth, he still wants to adopt you. He sees the greatness inside of you and wants to call you his own and for you to call him your father because he loves you so much. God is willing to help you go through the process to become the person he had created you to be since before you were in your mother's womb. You have to understand that there is nothing that you can do that would cause Him to take His love away from you.

Ephesians 1:5 reads, "God decided in advance to adopt us into his own family by bringing us to himself through Jesus Christ. This is what he wanted to do, and it gave him great pleasure."

It gives God great pleasure to adopt you by way of his son Jesus Christ. He wanted to do this. No one twisted his arm or forced him to make this decision. He knew that you needed him to make it through this life. He knew that you needed Jesus Christ to continually intercede for you. He knew that you needed the Holy Spirit to help counsel, comfort and guide you along the way. He knew that you needed the Trinity because there is no way that you are able to make up for your wrongs on your own.

Unlike what the kids said on the Food Network show, you do not have to redeem yourself. You do not have to redeem yourself because thanks to the love of God YOU ARE REDEEMED.

OBSERVATION:

Take time to think of how you view yourself. Do you feel like you have to make every wrong right before you can move on with your life? Do you find you are holding yourself hostage to the things of your past? Do you feel as though you can never be forgiven for things you have done? Do you believe that you were worth the investment of Christ's life in exchange for yours? It is necessary for you to make amends where the Holy Spirit shows you were wrong, but once you do your part you are now responsible to release yourself from that infraction. Romans 8:1 reads, "So now there is no condemnation for those who belong to Christ Jesus." Once you have been adopted into God's family you are no longer allowed to not forgive yourself or others for that matter. You have been forgiven the moment that you accepted Christ as your savior. All things for you have been made new and repentance will keep you in that new place of being at peace with your relationship with God. But it is your choice to receive that truth. Think about it. Look at your life and see what it is saying about who you are in the area of being REDEEMED.

PETITION:

Dear Lord,

You are forthcoming! Forgive me for not always believing that I am redeemed. Thank you for letting me know that I am redeemed. Help me to remember each day that I AM REDEEMED.

In Jesus' name, Amen.

D.R.O.P. #19

You Are...

RESPONSIBLE

DEFINITION:

RESPONSIBLE: (*adjective*) answerable or accountable, as for something within one's power, control, or management (often followed by to or for); involving accountability or responsibility, as in having the power to control or manage; chargeable with being the author, cause or occasion of something.

REFLECTION:

Being a responsible person is something that we all should strive to become if we are not that already. In my opinion, I believe that being a responsible person is a learned behavior that is developed over time. Unfortunately, those of us who may not have been taught how to take responsibility for ourselves at a younger age may be struggling with the idea of being accountable for something or someone at our current, or mature age.

In Proverbs 22:6, the scripture reads, "Train up a child in the way he should go; even when he is old he will not depart from it."

Reading this scripture speaks more to me than just about training up your child in the things of God (which is of upmost importance) but also as it pertains to everyday life practices such as: how to clean up after yourself, how to be a good sport, how to handle laundry, how to make your bed, how to cook basic meals, how to be polite and respectful toward others, how to manage your allowance, how to take responsibility for your actions. The list can continue. These are all practices that in the end will help a child be responsible up until their future as an adult.

As adults, it is up to us to measure what level of responsibility we can take on in our lives. We must be careful not to take on tasks that we are not able to be accountable for in that moment. For example, if you already have a full list of things to do, then taking on another responsibility that you truly do not have time to do is not wise, especially if someone else is relying on you to do it. It is important to be honest with how much you can manage. This is part of being responsible. Know what you can and cannot do at this moment in your life. And be careful not to take on things just to please others as you will find yourself overdrawn, stressed out and possibly resentful. This is when you learn to say, "No."

"No" is a powerful word. I have heard many people emphasize that "No" is a complete sentence—meaning there is no requirement for you to give reason behind your response unless you choose to do so. And all of this sounds good when pertaining to responding to other people, but when it comes to responding to God, "No" is not necessarily the best answer. The truth is that many times what God will ask for you to do will seem like it is too far from your reach or that it will require too much time that you just do not have. So instead of responding, "Yes" to Him, you say, "No," because you feel that you do not have the time, energy or possibly the capability to do what he has called for you to do. But what you must understand is that God will never tell you to do something you are incapable of doing.

Philippians 4:13 reads, "For I can do everything through Christ, who gives me strength."

This scripture was pertaining to being content in all situations. But it can also be interpreted just as it is written. You can do everything you need to do with the help of Christ who will give you the strength and the endurance that you need to complete the task ahead. And from my experience, if you say, "Yes" to his will, you will find that he will show you how to make time to accomplish that thing in which he has assigned you to do. And if you lean on him for help, you will find yourself with energy that you did not even know that you had. He gives you grace to manage the assignment. God has called you to be a responsible person (a steward). And he only calls those to be stewards if he finds you to be faithful and trustworthy.

I Corinthians 4:2 reads, "Now a person who is put in charge as a manager must be faithful."

Certainly if God has called you to be an overseer of something be it a book, business, household, or what have you, then he sees you as one who is faithful. You will find that being faithful is a requirement and not a recommendation. He also says that if you are faithful over little, he will then make you a ruler over much (Matthew 25:23). This is where your good stewardship becomes rewarded. God is pleased when his children take on his designated tasks and are productive by bringing that thing to its fullest potential. This is part of our duty as a believer in Christ. And God has found you to be one that he can count on to complete what He has instructed you to do. He is just waiting for a "Yes" because he believes that you are trustworthy and that YOU ARE RESPONSIBLE.

OBSERVATION:

Take time to think of how you view yourself. Do you take on assignments that you know are overtaxing? Do you do things to please others even though you know you don't have the time or desire to do them? Are you someone that people can rely on to complete a task? If you had to describe yourself, would the word "responsible" be a part of the description? Do you find yourself making excuses as to why you cannot stay committed to a thing? Have you been told by God to do something that you have still yet to do? Do you know why you are reluctant to do it? Remember that God will make a way even if it appears there is no way to get a thing done. Philippians 2:13 says, "For God is working in you, giving you the desire and the power to do what pleases him." If you have not done so already, then consider allowing God to work in you. What do you have to lose? Think about it. Look at your life and see what it is saying about who you are in the area of being RESPONSIBLE.

PETITION:

Dear Lord,

You are radiant! Forgive me for not always believing that I am responsible. Thank you for letting me know that I am responsible. Help me to remember each day that I AM RESPONSIBLE.

In Jesus' name, Amen.

D.R.O.P. #20

You Are...

PATIENT

DEFINITION:

PATIENT: (*adjective*) bearing provocation, annoyance, misfortune, delay, hardship, pain, etc., with fortitude and calm and without complaint, anger, or the like.; quietly and steadily persevering or diligent, especially in detail or exactness.

REFLECTION:

Being patient is not always an easy task. For many of us, it is something that is not part of our self-description. On many occasions I think we all can honestly say that we have admitted to not having patience or having a lack of patience. A popular saying that came out not too long ago was, "Ain't nobody got time for that." This could also help with the lack of patience mindset. I know for me, when I make it personal and say, "I ain't got time for this," (excuse the improper grammar but to me it makes the statement more real) I'm saying this is taking too much of my time and although it may be something I want, it is not something I am willing to put time in to do or it also may mean that this is not worth my time, therefore, I'm not going to focus on that thing right now or ever. We all have the power to choose what we have time for and what we do not have time for. This will then determine what we will decide to use our patience on. The question is, is it worth the wait?

To wait means to postpone or delay something in expectation. So while you wait, you have an expectation that keeps you wanting to hear or see what is to come. Depending on what you are in expectation for can determine how long you are willing to wait. If you become anxious, then the wait will seem too long, but if you become patient, then the wait will seem more endurable. When it comes to waiting on something that you truly desire, then gaining patience is a must. There is no room for excuses. And in the process of waiting and being patient, you have to do this while being calm and without complaining. You must be diligent, because diligence is what will keep you in the process.

Being diligent means that you are persistent in doing a thing; you are constantly making sure that you are committed even when you do not feel like it. So even though you may feel like complaining while you are waiting, you do not. You may feel like getting upset and irritated during the wait, but you remain calm and joyful in expectation of something good. Waiting and being patient is not for the weak, it is only for the strong.

Psalm 27:14 reads, "Wait patiently for the Lord. Be brave and courageous. Yes, wait patiently for the Lord."

Preluding to this verse, David was speaking of his enemies surrounding him and how he was trusting in the Lord to protect him. David was encouraged to be brave and courageous and to wait on the Lord. God is always worth the wait. When he says that he is going to do something then waiting on him is worth your time. And during the wait God is commanding you to be strong, to be brave, to be courageous because he knows that the wait is not easy but it is possible and that in the end when He shows up to fight your battle you will come out victorious.

We will all go through battles in this life. One major battle will be the battle of our mind. Thoughts will come into our mind and a battle will begin. We will have thought rivals such as: Doubt vs Faith. Fear vs Courage. Life vs Death. Health vs Sickness. Thoughts will try to come in and flood our minds to the point that we feel like we are drowning and want to give up on the good fight of faith (1 Timothy 6:12). But giving up is not an option for a believer in Christ because a believer in Christ always has hope and hope is what keeps us anchored in faith and faith is what keeps us trusting in God's promise. And if we trust in God's promise, then we know that we can count on him to come through. If we are assured that God will follow through on his word then we are able to bear all of the challenges that may come and do so in joy because we know that in the end we will have what we have been waiting for.

James 1:2-4 reads, "Dear brothers and sisters, when troubles of any kind come your way, consider it an opportunity for great joy. For you know that when your faith is tested, your endurance has a chance to grow. So let it grow, for when your endurance is fully developed, you will be perfect and complete, needing nothing."

Endurance is the same thing as patience. This scripture lets us know that in times of trouble we should wait it out in joy because in the end our patience level will grow. And when our patience is fully developed, then we are set to handle this life because every day of our life will require patience; patience with our neighbor, patience at the drive thru, patience with Amazon, patience with technical difficulties, patience with our kids, patience with our spouse, patience, patience, patience. So as it relates to having time for a thing, remember that you have the power to decide what you will wait on. And if it is something that God has promised, then it is worth the wait because God is faithful in keeping his word. Plus anything that comes from God is going to be good! You came from God by way of a woman and you were worth the wait. And when you think about it, you are a product of endurance, therefore, YOU ARE PATIENT.

OBSERVATION:

Take time to think of how you view yourself. Do you see yourself as one who can wait on something that you really desire? Do you find that you complain when something does not come as soon as you would like it to come? Do you find yourself giving up too easy? Do you think that you lack patience based on what you have and have not completed or received this far in life? Accomplishments in life take time. There are really no overnight success stories. It may appear that way because we only hear about a thing when it is complete. But rest assured there was a process to that persons' accomplishment. The question becomes, are you willing to make time to work toward what you desire? Is it worth your time? Think about it. Look at your life and see what it is saying about who you are in the area of being PATIENT.

PETITION:
Dear Lord,

You are matchless! Forgive me for not always believing that I am patient. Thank you for letting me know that I am patient. Help me to remember each day that I AM PATIENT.

In Jesus' name, Amen.

D.R.O.P. #21

You Are...

STRONG

DEFINITION:

STRONG: (*adjective*) having, showing, or able to exert great bodily or muscular power; physically vigorous or robust; mentally powerful or vigorous.

REFLECTION:

Have you ever felt weak physically, mentally and spiritually? I know I have and still sometimes do even in my present state of life. Sometimes things can hit you hard mentally that you feel too weak physically to even get out of bed. Sometimes you cannot even find the strength to get dressed, comb your hair, brush your teeth, wash your face, all the basics, due to feeling heartbroken or saddened. Other times it could be complete laziness that keeps you from doing those basic things which in the end, still has to deal with your mindset. Why are you feeling lazy? That becomes the question.

I remember when I went through my first miscarriage and how that made me feel. My husband was at work at the time so he was not able to go to the ultrasound appointment with me. When I found out that we were about to go through the process of a miscarriage, I began to cry in the doctor's office, called my husband as I walked to the car, then drove straight home. When I got home, I went straight to my bedroom, closed the blinds, laid on my bed, threw the covers over my head and continued to cry. It was automatic. I did not plan to react that way I just did. I was grieved in my spirit and instead of sand (like in the Bible days) I threw blankets over my head as if to say, "Don't bother me world, my shop of life is closed for today, I am in sorrow and might reopen again tomorrow but please don't count on it."

I am sure somewhere in there I did say a prayer because I am someone who constantly talks to God. I knew deep in my heart that God was going to walk me and my husband through this and that we would be okay, but in that moment I was heartbroken. Going back to that day, I remember my husband immediately left work and came home early. He saw me in the state I was in, uncovered me and said, "No, we are not going to do this." He then encouraged me to get up, get dressed and go somewhere with him. He gave me a pep talk like he typically does and in that moment it was helpful, but my heart still hurt (as I'm sure his did too). Spiritually I felt weak because although I knew God was with me, I did not feel like I had the strength to fight the good fight of faith. But eventually I did get up and continued to fight.

When it comes to us as women, I believe that God has given us strength like no other. He has given us the ability to handle pressures that men could not handle and vice versa. But in this case, I am speaking of us as women and how powerful God has made us to be. He knew the hardships that we would go through as a woman, nurturer, significant other, help meet. And he knew that we would be able to withstand those circumstances and come out on top.

In Proverbs 31:25, it reads, "She is clothed with strength and dignity, and she laughs without fear of the future." This speaks of a woman that we are able to draw from as an example of what we are able to obtain individually and as a community of women. Yes, we need each other to help get us through moments in time where we all can relate. Because the truth is that what you are going through, others are going through or have already passed that course. And we need each other to be reminded that just like the Proverbs 31 woman, you are clothed in strength and dignity! You keep your head held up high even through the tough and shameful moments. You laugh even when times are hard.

2 Corinthians 12:9-11 reads, "Each time he said, 'My grace is all you need. My power works best in weakness.' So now I am glad to boast about my weaknesses, so that the power of Christ can work through me. That's why I take pleasure in my weaknesses, and in the insults, hardships, persecutions, and troubles that I suffer for Christ. For when I am weak, then I am strong." This scripture lets me know that you do not have to pretend to have it all together. You do not have to pretend that you are not weak at certain times in your life. If you are able to confess your weaknesses, then God is able to perfect your strength. Your weakness is an area that can be worked out. It can be worked out because you are a child of God and as His child He will not allow you to go through a situation without gaining strength from it.

Being able to survive in this world requires physical, mental and spiritual strength, all of which you acquire. You are not in this life alone. God is always fighting on your behalf. Christ is always interceding on your behalf. The Holy Spirit has been sent to be with you on your behalf. You have the trinity on your side. And many times the help of the Father will come by way of your neighbor, your spouse, your co-worker, a stranger. Do not reject your help because it does not look like the help you expected. And know that you are able to go through this life of yours because you were built for this pressure. God said that he will not put more on you than you can bear (1 Corinthians 10:13). You have it within you to come out victorious. You have what it takes to go through the dark situations and in the end see the light because YOU ARE STRONG.

OBSERVATION:

Take time to think of how you view yourself. How many pounds can you lift? How many Bible scriptures can you recall? How many opinions of others can you endure? What is your strength level? Do you find yourself weak in the areas of physical, mental and spiritual? If you do, then know that it is okay. It is okay to be weak because that is where you will be made strong. You will be made strong only if you submit your weakness unto the Lord so that you can receive his help. Do not think that you have to lift the weights of life on your own. You have someone who has been sent to "spot" you. Like a weight trainer does with his trainee, God will do more for you. He will see when you feel weak and he will help you lift the weight up. We all need help to make it through this life. And just because you need help does not mean that you are weak. That is not the truth. Strong individuals know when they need help and are not ashamed to ask for assistance. Think about it. Look at your life and see what it is saying about who you are in the area of being STRONG.

PETITION:
Dear Lord,

You are terrific! Forgive me for not always believing that I am strong. Thank you for letting me know that I am strong. Help me to remember each day that I AM STRONG.

In Jesus' name, Amen.

D.R.O.P. #22

You Are...

ENOUGH

DEFINITION:

ENOUGH: (*adjective*) adequate for the want or need; sufficient for the purpose or to satisfy desire.

REFLECTION:

There are some things in life that I can speak about more than others, and I am sure the same is true for you. This one area of believing that you are enough is one of them for me. Being that I had struggled with insecurity and low self-esteem for most of my life, I have come to know what it means to not feel like you are enough in every area of life. From relationships, to ministry, to employment, to pursuing purpose, the list continues. There was always a thought that would pop up and linger influencing me to believe that I was not able to fulfill the position that I was in. Even now, being a wife and a mother, there have been times where the question comes up and the thought thrives in my head, "Am I enough?" And if I am not careful that thought can rule my behavior causing me to want to give up in the area where I do not feel sufficient but I cannot ignore the question rather I must address it.

Let us go back to the question, "Am I enough?" I know that we would love to instantly respond, "Yes! You are enough girl! Don't let the enemy tell you any different!" And that response is in fact warranted for encouragement purposes but what I have found is that it is important to respond in a way that causes the other person to identify why they are feeling that way. A proper response would be, "What would make you think that you are not enough?" And then let the process roll on from there.

When dealing with insecurity, you want to have open-ended questions versus closed-ended statements. Open-ended questions will allow the thoughts to be processed while close ended statements will close off the conversation that is necessary to get to the core of how one is feeling. For example, in answering the question as a wife, you may respond that you do not feel like you are enough because you lack in the areas of communication and intimacy which you know is necessary for a marriage to be strong. From that response the next question could be, "Why do you feel you have a hard time communicating and being intimate with your spouse?" The discussion could then go deeper and hopefully things will be revealed to help you as a wife be more comfortable with communicating and being intimate with your husband. In all honesty, if we as wives are not fulfilling those two specific needs of our mates, then I would venture to say that we are not doing our best as wives.

This leads me to the feeling of not being enough can stem from us not believing that we are performing at our best. And sometimes that belief is true—we are not giving our all to the target at hand. Other times the belief is false. You are giving your absolute best but the response that you are receiving from the target is saying to you that your best is not good enough and that you need to give more. This is where you have to assess the situation and question if whether or not your best is truthfully not your best or if you are simply being exploited. If the answer is yes to not giving your best and being exploited then the next questions become, "Why are you not giving your best?" and "Why are you putting up with exploitation?" This is where confronting the real issue comes into play. You are worth confrontation. This part of the process may be uncomfortable, but it is necessary for exposure so that you can get closure in this area.

We have to understand that in most cases we are not going to be automatic experts in our roles that we have been given as a wife, mother, business woman, employee, role model, etc. This is true because we have been constructed to learn more as we grow. As we grow, we will begin to mature in that assigned role and gain wisdom that then becomes identified as expertise. Wisdom will get you to a place where you will be able to identify the areas of which you need improvement to become/ continue to be the best you in that area of life. And in that process of gaining wisdom, you will need to extend yourself the grace that is needed to forgive when you do not always hit the mark of being sufficient. You will also need to have an understanding that your capacity to fulfill your assigned role may start off small in the beginning, but with time it will expand if you allow yourself to learn along the way and apply what you have learned to that area of life.

Proverbs 4:7 reads, "Getting wisdom is the wisest thing you can do! And whatever else you do, develop good judgment."

Good judgment is equivalent to being understanding. It is important that as you gain wisdom you also gain an understanding as to why you may not feel like you have what it takes to fulfill your roles in life. The answer to that feeling is going to take a lot out of you as you begin to unfold the layers that are covering your reason for insecurity and low self-esteem. Give yourself time to process what you discover. And as you process that information in the end you should gain the revelation that if you have been given that role in life, then you are the perfect person for the job, it just may be that you need more training along the way. Just like when you are hired for employment, you may have the basic skills to perform your duties but there is always more to learn as you go which is where your employer will give you specific training to be the best in the position that you have taken on. Through this training (growing in wisdom) you will begin to feel more equipped to walk out the assignment given because YOU ARE ENOUGH.

OBSERVATION:

Take time to think of how you view yourself. Are you expecting more out of yourself than what should be expected at this time in your life? Are you comparing yourself to others and thinking that you could never rise where they are? Do you know that in order to be the best in any area in life that it is going to take time? Have you forsaken the process that is necessary to get you to know and believe that you are sufficient for the role? Hebrews 5:11-12 reads, "There is much more we would like to say about this, but it is difficult to explain, especially since you are spiritually dull and don't seem to listen. You have been believers so long now that you ought to be teaching others. Instead, you need someone to teach you again the basic things about God's word. You are like babies who need milk and cannot eat solid food." Do you think that perhaps you are not feeling enough because you have taken on a role that you are not able to digest (handle) at this time? Perhaps you did not learn from your experiences and are now still at a level where you feel insufficient. Perhaps you may need to go back to the basics and mature from there. Think about it. Look at your life and see what it is saying about who you are in the area of being ENOUGH.

PETITION:
Dear Lord,

You are incredible! Forgive me for not always believing that I am enough. Thank you for letting me know that I am enough. Help me to remember each day that I AM ENOUGH.

In Jesus' name, Amen.

D.R.O.P. #23

You Are...

ACCEPTED

DEFINITION:

ACCEPTED: (*adjective*) generally approved; usually regarded as normal, right, etc.

REFLECTION:

Recently I was watching an old episode from a show titled, "This Is Us." In this particular episode, the focus was on the two brothers, Kevin and Randall, and their relationship. As a quick backdrop, Kevin is Caucasian and Randall is African American. Randall and Kevin were born on the same day. Randall was left at a fire station and brought to the hospital where Kevin's parents decided to adopt him after finding out they had lost one of their babies (the parents were expecting triplets). During their childhood both Randall and Kevin felt some form of rejection. Randall explained to Kevin that he felt like Kevin never wanted him around. He stated that in the 36 years they had known each other, Kevin never claimed him to be his brother until their recent physical altercation in public. Kevin explained that he felt like Randall was the favorite of his mom's which deprived Kevin of the love that he needed from her. Both of the brother's expressed feeling rejected which later turned into resentment. In the end, all they wanted was to be accepted.

Acceptance is a major need in everyone's life. If we do not feel accepted, then we do not feel wanted. If we do not feel wanted, then we do not feel needed. If we do not feel needed, then we begin to question why we even exist. If we begin to question why we even exist, then we may fall into the trap of giving up. If we fall into the trap of giving up, then we may find ourselves in a place of self-harm. If we find ourselves in a place of self-harm, then we will need to reach out to someone for help. If we need to reach out to someone for help, then we must be able to receive the help so that we can overcome our thoughts so that we can choose to live. We must choose to live even when we feel like others could care less if we lived or died. We must choose to live because Christ died so that we may live. We must choose to live because that is the reason why we were born.

We were born to live and be productive. Genesis 1:28 reads, "Then God blessed them and said, "Be fruitful and multiply. Fill the earth and govern it. Reign over the fish in the sea, the birds in the sky, and all the animals that scurry along the ground." This scripture lets us know that we have the ability to produce. To produce means to bring something forth, to bring something into existence. But how can we bring something into existence that is beneficial if we do not feel like we ourselves want to exist? I am reminded of Maslow's Hierarchy of Needs theory.

Maslow's Hierarchy of Needs theory states that there are five essential needs of every human being: (1) Physiological Needs, (2) Safety needs, (3) Love and belonging, (4) Esteem, (5) Self-actualization.

You can see that acceptance (love and belonging) is one of the five needs. As a matter of fact, it lands right in the middle which can be viewed as the core of the needs. And when something is the core, it is the most essential. In order for any of the needs to be met, the need of love and belonging has to take root. The truth is that everyone wants to be loved whether they admit it or not. Everyone wants to feel like they belong. No one was born to be rejected or live life alone. We were all born to live life with others who can help us be the best that we can be which brings us to the need we are all striving toward which is self-actualization.

There are so many self- help books out here in this world because there is a need for people to believe that they were born for a reason and that they do not need to give up on who they are. I know that I hear a lot of church messages on knowing who you are, your value and your need to be the best you because you are needed in this life. Someone is waiting for you to rise to the occasion so that they can receive the help that they need to rise up and produce as well. We are in a cycle of life. What you go through and come out of, you then help others go through and come out of and so the "pay-it-forward" cycle continues.

It is important that you know that you are not a reject or a disappointment. You are not without purpose or born without a reason. Whether you have been abandoned or neglected, abused or misused, rejected or afflicted, overlooked or forgotten, the truth remains that God sees you and that He knows you. God has predestined you for a purpose. God has chosen you to be his child.

Romans 15:5-7 reads, "May God, who gives this patience and encouragement, help you live in complete harmony with each other, as is fitting for followers of Christ Jesus. Then all of you can join together with one voice, giving praise and glory to God, the Father of our Lord Jesus Christ. Therefore, accept each other just as Christ has accepted you so that God will be given glory."

You have been chosen by God so that you can follow Christ, love others and become united so that in the end you will give praise and glory to God. You will give God the glory he requires once you have the knowing that YOU ARE ACCEPTED.

OBSERVATION:
Take time to think of how you view yourself. Do you find yourself constantly feeling like you are the outsider looking in? Do you find yourself uncomfortable around others? Is there any resentment in your heart toward others who may have rejected you? Are you able to look into the mirror and tell yourself that you are important? Do you find yourself reaching for others to acknowledge you? You must understand not everyone will see you in the light that you are supposed to be seen. Some people may look at you with distaste or not look at you at all because you bring no interest to them. But this is not what you are to

concentrate on. You are not going to be welcomed everywhere that you go. Even Jesus experienced this when he said in Luke 4:24, "But I tell you the truth, no prophet is accepted in his own hometown." You will experience rejection because it is a part of life. But even though you are rejected by few it does not authorize you to give up and never reach those who will accept you. Think about it. Look at your life and see what it is saying about who you are in the area of being ACCEPTED.

PETITION:

Dear Lord,

You are great! Forgive me for not always believing that I am accepted. Thank you for letting me know that I am accepted. Help me to remember each day that I AM ACCEPTED.

In Jesus' name, Amen.

D.R.O.P. #24

You Are...

PURPOSEFUL

DEFINITION:

PURPOSEFUL: (*adjective*) having a purpose; determined; resolute; full of meaning; significant

REFLECTION:

In the world that we are living in at this moment in time, I think if reviewed carefully we can see that there is a lack of purposeful living in many people's lives. With the increase of depression, suicide, homicide, mass shootings and the like, you can see that there is a sense of lowliness that is taking place.

Just recently my husband shared a story of a man who killed his wife, who was expecting their third child, and his two daughters, all because he wanted to leave his family and be with another woman. This story caused me to think back when the recession hit and millions lost their jobs. I remember hearing stories of the head of households killing their families and themselves as they did not know how they were going to live without a sure financial foundation. My heart aches when I hear these stories of death, hopelessness and defeat, especially when a child is involved who is not even given the right to decide for their own life.

If only we could fully understand just how significant we are as a people. If only we could truly understand and believe that we are full of meaning. If only we could get to the point that we are determined to survive and to live a life worth living whether our surrounding conditions agree with us or not. This does not have to be far from our reach if only we decide to follow Jesus and get to know who He is and begin to trust the goodness of God.

Romans 8:28 reads, "And we know that God causes everything to work together for the good of those who love God and are called according to his purpose for them."

If you are one of those who love God, then you must know that God will cause everything that you are going through to work out for the good of your life. So even in the midst of trials God said that He will work it all out for you. This means that if you are going through a financial slump, marital problems, trouble raising your children, loss of a loved one, any situation that seems like it is overbearing, God says that he will work it out for your good. If only you trust and believe and submit to the purpose that he has for your life.

Through submission to God we will find peace in every storm. God has a way of quieting the noise when we get into his presence through prayer, song and dance. Yes, dance! I know that I am not a dancer. And to be honest when I clap and move my feet at the same time I get confused and it just becomes a mess. This is why in church during praise and worship, I sometimes have to stop moving to try and regain some kind of rhythm so that I will not embarrass my husband too much. Even though I cannot dance much, I still know that if I get into the presence of God through dance there is a shift that takes place in my mindset. I begin to forget about my troubles and concentrate on his goodness. And no bad thing can stand against his goodness. During times of worship, praise and adoration, you will find that it is the best time to cast all of your cares.

1 Peter 5:7 reads, "Give all your worries and cares to God, for he cares about you."

God cares about you. He desires to take all of your worries and concerns. He does not want you to worry about a thing because he has only your best interest in mind. But you have to learn to let go of those weights in life that keep trying to hold you down and allow God to lift them off of you. This is something that must be done because there is purpose for you to fulfill.

We all have the same purposeful outcome: to bring praise and glory to God. So whether you believe that God has called you to work in fashion, music, entertainment, fitness, education, ministry, whatever it may be, the purpose is to do the work with the intent of honoring God and leading others to Christ. You must remember that your life is full of meaning. Even during the toughest of times. During all the heartache and suffering, God promises that he will work it all out for your good because your life is worth living. Your life is worth fighting for because YOU ARE PURPOSEFUL.

OBSERVATION:

Take time to think of how you view yourself. Do you believe that your life is worth living? Are you having a hard time determining your purpose in life? Can you agree that in any field of work you choose that in the end the purpose is to bring God praise and glory? Do you trust that God will work out every situation for your good? Do you know that no matter what has taken place in your life that you are still full of meaning? Looking back at David in the Bible, he went through a lot of afflictions which were brought upon himself and others that were not. But in the end he commanded his soul to praise the Lord. He danced like there was no one to impress. He repented and got back up again because he knew that God still had a purpose to fulfill in his life. Can you say the same for yourself? Think about it. Look at your life and see what it is saying about who you are in the area of being PURPOSEFUL.

PETITION:

Dear Lord,

You are excellent! Forgive me for not always believing that I am purposeful. Thank you for letting me know that I am purposeful. Help me to remember each day that I AM PURPOSEFUL.

In Jesus' name, Amen.

D.R.O.P. #25

You Are...

COVERED

DEFINITION:

COVERED: (*verb-used with an object*) to be or serve as a covering for; extend over; rest on the surface of; to place something over or upon, as for protection, concealment, or warmth.; to provide with a covering or top.

REFLECTION:

For the past decade I have chosen to work in the group home field with teenagers. (Group homes are temporary placements for children who are in the foster care system.) As a facility manager in a group home, it is my job to communicate with the child's social worker to find out if they can have community passes; which basically is the ability to go outside and walk around the local community on their own. If they are able to go on a community pass, then they are given a specific amount of hours that they can be out on their own as well as a curfew.

A curfew is defined as a regulation requiring a person to be home at a certain prescribed time, as imposed by a parent on a child. A curfew is also set in each state to make sure that young civilians are not on the streets past a certain time at night. The way I like to see it is that a curfew is set in place for protection. Once an individual decides to dishonor their curfew time and stay out past the time given, that is the moment that they are no longer protected and have officially removed themselves from being covered.

Being covered is a blessing. And I am not speaking of being covered by placing a blanket over your body for warmth (although that is a blessing, too) but being covered as for protection and rest in knowing that you are being watched over by God.

Psalm 91:1 reads, "Those who live in the shelter of the Most High will find rest in the shadow of the Almighty."

There is a special rest that you will find when you decide to live in the covering of God. When you decide to trust God to be the head over your life, that will be the moment that you allow him to be the shelter that you need to make it through life's hardships. Shelter is necessary for protection from rain, winds, too much sun exposure, basically all the conditions of life that may come your way. Shelter is what gives the conditions of life a boundary, and boundaries are necessary for protection.

Many people do not want to have boundaries in their life, but boundaries are needed to make sure that certain lines will not be crossed that will cause harm to you. When you think of a boundary consider a sign that reads, "No trespassing." When you decide to place a "no trespassing" sign in your life, then you will find that people will stop dishonoring you and you also will stop dishonoring yourself. When you do not have boundaries set in place, then you have basically given approval for your life to be an open target. You have given permission for temptations to have their way in your life and lead you to sin. You have given the okay to not be protected in that area of life. This should not be so because you are royalty.

Consider royalty treatment. As a child of a king, you will find that they cannot go outside their palace without protection. They always have to have their bodyguard around to ensure their safety because children of the king are well-known and targets for destruction. There are people who want to purposefully destroy children of the king by either stealing from them because they are wealthy, killing them because they are enviable, and or destroying them because it will bring grief to the royal family. Many times the attack is not about the child, but about destroying the king's honor that is due to him. In this case you are the child and God is the king. Think about when tragedy strikes many times what arises is blame on God and disappointment in his "lack of protection." This resentment will lead to children stepping out of the covering of God by making up their own curfew, their own boundaries that fit their lifestyle. But in the end, when the covering has been removed and boundaries have been erased or stretched, you become an open target, and if you become an open target, then you will be subject to destruction. If you become destroyed then God will not be given the praise and glory that is due him.

John 10:10 reads, "The thief's purpose is to steal and kill and destroy. My purpose is to give them a rich and satisfying life." You can see that God is not the author of tragedy but Satan is and he loves to get you off course. This is why you must pay attention to the conditions of your life and assess how you are feeling in your soul. Assess if, at this moment, you are feeling vulnerable, weak, confused or if you have a sound mind. In

Luke 4:13 it reads, "When the devil had finished tempting Jesus, he left him until the next opportunity came." At all times you have to take time to assess your strength, assess your mindset. The enemy is observing you and looking for moments of weakness or busyness to approach you again. This is why you must make time for prayer and staying under the protection of God by acknowledging him in all things that you do. Allow him to be the top that you need in your life to prevent from being an open target. Honor the curfew and boundaries that he has set for your life. You are not too grown for protection. Remember, do not be consumed with worrying about the conditions of life but learn to find rest in knowing that as a child of the king YOU ARE COVERED.

OBSERVATION:

Take time to think of how you view yourself. Do you find yourself setting your own rules in your life? Do you find that your rules go against God's best interest for you? Have you ever felt as though you are too grown to have limits? When you are under the covering of God and are attentive to his voice, you will find that he will speak to you about what boundaries you need to place in your life as well as what time you need to be at home on a daily basis. God will give you these instructions through the aid of the Holy Spirit. The Holy Spirit will give you the inclination on when it is time to leave an environment (person, place or thing). This is why it is of upmost importance to stay in tune with the Holy Spirit because he serves as the voice of God giving you counseling, guidance and comfort (like a warm blanket). You are not too grown to make up your own mind without the consultation of God. Proverbs 3:5-6 reads, "Trust in the Lord with all your heart; do not depend on your own understanding. Seek his will in all you do, and he will show you which path to take." Are you seeking God's will in everything you do? Are you allowing him to direct your path and be the covering that you need? Think about it. Look at your life and see what it is saying about who you are in the area of being COVERED.

PETITION:
Dear Lord,

You are a way maker! Forgive me for not always believing that I am covered. Thank you for letting me know that I am covered. Help me to remember each day that I AM COVERED.

In Jesus' name, Amen.

D.R.O.P. #26

You Are...

RIGHTEOUS

DEFINITION:

RIGHTEOUS: (*adjective*) characterized by uprightness or morality; morally right or justifiable; acting in an upright, moral way; virtuous.

REFLECTION:

Romans 3:22 reads, "We are made right with God by placing our faith in Jesus Christ. And this is true for everyone who believes, no matter who we are."

No matter who you are, no matter what background you may come from, what nationality you represent, what shoe or pant size you wear, how tall you are, if your hair is curly or straight, no matter how people view you, if you have accepted Jesus Christ as your Lord and Savior and have placed your faith in Jesus Christ, then you are made right with God. You are now in position to live a life that is morally right and justifiable.

The beautiful thing about coming to know Christ as your Lord and Savior is that he will take time to teach you how to be an upstanding person. When you choose to make Christ your leader and follow him, you are choosing to learn from Christ and to glean from his character and ways. This gives you firsthand access into knowing how to be a person of integrity.

Integrity is something that cannot be purchased, imitated or faked. Integrity has to be learned and implemented in your daily lifestyle. Integrity is when you are able to adhere to moral and ethical principles even when you have opportunity for dishonest gain. Integrity requires honesty. When dealing with people in life one of the most important character traits that should be sought for is honesty. When you find someone who is honest then you are more than likely able to find trust within that person as well, and finding a person that you can trust brings pleasure.

Proverbs 16:13 reads, "The king is pleased with words from righteous lips; he loves those who speak honestly." Righteous lips are those that can be trusted to speak honestly. Honesty brings pleasure to the king. If you want to know how to please God, then learn how to be one who is honest.

1 Peter 3:10-12 reads, "For the Scriptures say, 'If you want to enjoy life and see many happy days, keep your tongue from speaking evil and your lips from telling lies. Turn away from evil and do good. Search for peace, and work to maintain it. The eyes of the Lord watch over those who do right, and his ears are open to their prayers. But the Lord turns his face against those who do evil.'"

This scripture lets us know that God will protect and listen to the prayers of those who live an upright lifestyle. God desires that you live an enjoyable long life but it will require a few things out of you that you are more than capable of producing. It will require three main things: (1) not speaking evil or telling lies, (2) turning away from evil, (3) seeking peace and keeping it.

You are able to do what is required of you because you have chosen to follow Christ who will lead you to a place of repentance when you miss the mark. No matter who you are, you are able to be free in Christ and tell him what your concerns and hiccups are in living a life that is upstanding. God is not asking you to be morally sound on your own. He understands that you will need to do it with the aid of Jesus Christ and the Holy Spirit. This is why your relationship with Jesus is so important because in order to be used by God he must trust that you can follow Christ. Because in Christ you will find the faith that you need to be a person of integrity. And integrity will only remain in you if you remain in Christ. John 15:4 says, "Remain in me, and I will remain in you. For a branch cannot produce fruit if it is severed from the vine, and you cannot be fruitful unless you remain in me." The only way that you will be able to produce this lifestyle of morals is if you choose to remain connected to the source, Jesus Christ. And it is only at this level that you can honestly say that YOU ARE RIGHTEOUS.

OBSERVATION:

Take time to think of how you view yourself. Do you see yourself as one that others can trust? When you look at your lifestyle can you honestly say that you are the same behind closed doors and in the public eye? Do you find that it is easier to tell the truth or a lie? Do you consider yourself to be a leader? Leaders are those who can be trusted to do the right thing while being followed by others. If a leader makes a wrong judgment call, then the leader is able to admit it to his/her followers so that they can know the importance of honesty and pressing forward to make better choices. You do not have to stay in a place of shame if you miss the mark of upholding your morals. God will not condemn you but convict you to learn from your error and do right the next opportunity that comes your way. Will you extend this same grace to others and yourself as a believer in Christ? Think about it. Look at your life and see what it is saying about who you are in the area of being RIGHTEOUS.

PETITION:

Dear Lord,

You are glorious! Forgive me for not always believing that I am righteous. Thank you for letting me know that I am righteous. Help me to remember each day that I AM RIGHTEOUS.

In Jesus' name, Amen.

D.R.O.P. #27

You Are...

WISE

DEFINITION:

WISE: (*adjective*) having the power of discerning and judging properly as to what is true or right; possessing discernment, judgment, or discretion.; characterized by or showing such power; judicious or prudent; possessed of or characterized by scholarly knowledge or learning; learned; erudite.

REFLECTION:

I remember back in my college days how I made decisions that were not exactly the best for my life. As a matter of fact, they were downright dumb choices on my part that had some lasting effects of insecurity, shame and regret. No need to mention that most of these lasting effects came from choices that dealt with the opposite sex. I could use the excuse of being young, but the truth is that I knew what I was doing was not morally right. I also knew that I was wiser than that, but at the time I chose to put my wisdom to the side to make room for my flesh nature to have some freedom. But in the end, that freedom only turned into bondage that took years for me to break free from, thanks be to God!

Have you ever put your wisdom to the side so that you can live in that moment? So many of us falter in this area of living life to the fullest and living a life of freedom. We think that living our best life means doing what we want to do versus doing what God has created us to do; which is not right. I know that for me personally, the greatest freedom I have ever felt was the freedom I found in living for Christ and staying pure before him. That is the place where I have personally found the greatest joy.

When you live for Christ and live to please him, freedom automatically comes with that decision. Because in doing right by God, you will find that you will receive so many great inheritances. One of the inheritances is wisdom. Some would say that wisdom is comparable to wealth but the truth is that wisdom is on a value system of its own.

Ecclesiastes 7:11-12 reads, "Wisdom is even better when you have money. Both are a benefit as you go through life. Wisdom and money can get you almost anything, but only wisdom can save your life." This scripture is so profound to me. Wisdom and money are both beneficial to your life when it comes to accruing things that you want or need, but in the end wisdom out-weighs money because it can save your life.

Think about how many times your life has been saved by making that one wise decision. You said no to his proposal. You did not stay the night at that stranger's house. You did not go out that night even though all your friends were encouraging you to do so. You chose to not move out of state. You did not drive even though you were only a little bit tipsy. You chose to keep your kids at home versus in that daycare. So many decisions you have made that has spared your life and others all on the count of having good judgment. You calculated your thoughts, you consulted the Holy Spirit, you sought wise counsel, you then made a decision that had the power to completely alter your life.

From the smallest to the biggest, each step that you take in life will require not only money but wisdom. Money may take you there, but wisdom will keep you there if that is where you belong. Wisdom will say, "I know I have invested a lot of money and time into this person, place or thing but it is time to part ways or it is time now to go to the next level." Wisdom will guide you into all truth.

Proverbs 3:15-18 reads, "Wisdom is more precious than rubies; nothing you desire can compare with her. She offers you long life in her right hand, and riches and honor in her left. She will guide you down delightful paths; all her ways are satisfying. Wisdom is a tree of life to those who embrace her; happy are those who hold her tightly." Are you happy in life? If not, then perhaps you are lacking wisdom. I know for me I am most unhappy when I do not know what choice to make. From a small decision like picking out what to eat to a big decision like deciding what step to take next in a relationship, when I do not know what choice to make, I find myself irritated and scrambled which in the end leads me to not feeling happy. If you make an unwise decision, you will find yourself unsatisfied with your choice. This is why it is important to take your time in deciding what to do.

Do not feel pressured to answer anyone on the spot. You have the right to take your time. The great thing about wisdom is that many times you will know in advance what you will and will not approve in your life based on the wisdom you have gained from reading God's word and knowing him personally. This is the advantage that we have as believers in Jesus Christ. We have the advantage of seeking his face for counseling and direction. We do not have to make this decision on our own. James 1:5 reads, "If you need wisdom, ask our generous God, and he will give it to you. He will not rebuke you for asking."

It is wise to ask God for wisdom in every area of our lives. You need it because the choices that you make may not seem wise to others but that is why you have to know God's voice for yourself. He will give you instructions personally for your life that others may not understand. Take Noah, for example. He heard God's voice and started to build an arch to prep for a rainstorm while it was still sunny outside. Many laughed at him for the decision that he was making but in the end Noah had the last laugh because wisdom saved his life!

You also have the power to save your life by the choices you make today. If you have not accepted Jesus Christ as your personal Lord and Savior, then now is the time to do it. If you have already accepted Jesus Christ as your Lord and Savior but have found yourself living a life contrary to what you know is morally right, then now is the time to repent and rededicate your life back to Christ. You are more than capable of assessing your life and making the right decision that leads to true freedom because YOU ARE WISE.

OBSERVATION:

Take time to think of how you view yourself. Do you consider yourself a person of good judgment? Do you find it hard to tell if something is good or bad for you? Do you find yourself agreeing more with the way of the world than the way of the Lord? James 3:13-16 reads, " If you are wise and understand God's ways, prove it by living an honorable life, doing good works with the humility that comes from wisdom. But if you are bitterly jealous and there is selfish ambition in your heart, don't cover up the truth with boasting and lying. For jealousy and selfishness are not God's kind of wisdom. Such things are earthly, unspiritual, and demonic. For wherever there is jealousy and selfish ambition, there you will find disorder and evil of every kind." Based on this scripture, you will find that worldly wisdom will lead to disorder and evil doings but godly wisdom will lead to order and good works. Which type of wisdom are you operating under? Think about it. Look at your life and see what it is saying about who you are in the area of being WISE.

PETITION:

Dear Lord,

You are generous! Forgive me for not always believing that I am wise. Thank you for letting me know that I am wise. Help me to remember each day that I AM WISE.

In Jesus' name, Amen.

D.R.O.P. #28

You Are...

CAPABLE

DEFINITION:

CAPABLE: (*adjective*) having power and ability; efficient; competent.

REFLECTION:

Self-doubt is one of the most destructive weapons that the enemy will try to hand you. The picture that just came to mind was someone handing you a gun and instructing you to point it to your head and pull the trigger. In the end, you are the one who does the act of taking your own life. Self-doubt will rob you of living the best life that God has planned for you to live. It will cause you to miss out on great opportunities. It will cause you to say no before giving you a chance to prove that you can do it. Self-doubt is selfish.

Being selfish is defined as caring only for oneself. You are concerned primarily with your own interests, benefits, welfare, etc., regardless of others. To think of self-doubt in this way can seem kind of harsh. I think this is because self-doubt has been cradled much like a baby. We have been trained to cater to self-doubt as something that needs to be given attention and comfort. Many of us have experienced self-doubt and found ourselves in a position of feeling like a victim. We magnify the thought that we cannot do something to the point that we fall prey to our state of mind and are devoured by the lies of the enemy. This leads us to not fulfilling the assignment that God has given us which not only affects our life but those whom we were assigned to help. This is where the selfish part takes place.

You were not created just to walk around and be cute. You were created to walk around and be the change that people need to see, hear and touch. You were created to help others come to know Christ. You were created to be an example of God's goodness. You were created to bring God praise and glory to his name. But how can you do any of this if you decide to cut your life short by doubting yourself and your capabilities? God needs for you to stand up to the enemy and let him know that you are not afraid of entering into the life that God has designed for you to walk in. God needs for you to prove that you are stable and able to stand on his word of faith and act on it.

James 1:5-8 reads, "If you need wisdom, ask our generous God, and he will give it to you. He will not rebuke you for asking. But when you ask him, be sure that your faith is in God alone. Do not waver, for a person with divided loyalty is as unsettled as a wave of the sea that is blown and tossed by the wind. Such people should not expect to receive anything from the Lord. Their loyalty is divided between God and the world, and they are unstable in everything they do."

This scripture discusses being double-minded. You are unable to make up your mind as to whether you can or cannot do it. You ask God for wisdom but now you are unsure if you should have asked him for wisdom. Maybe you should have asked him for peace? Your faith is wavering where God is not able to answer your prayer because you did not believe that you would receive it when you prayed. When you are not sure what to think, you are now considered unstable and unstable people are not reliable.

Think about going into a business relationship with someone. When you are about to spend your time, money and energy into something that has great potential of being profitable you want to know that without a shadow of a doubt your business partner is all in. They are not just going to work with you part time but they are going to invest themselves fully into what you have. This reminds me of the television show, Shark Tank. The investors want to know if the business owner is 100% sold out to working their company. They want to know that the business owner knows their financial information. You have to be completely sold out to your vision. This is proof of not being in a position of self-doubt.

When you are sold out to the vision that God has given you, you do not have time to entertain the idea of not being able to do what he has called for you to do. Will doubtful thoughts pop up in your mind while doing the will of God? Of course. But you do not have to entertain those thoughts. You can confront them by speaking to God about how you are feeling and what you are thinking and in the end let him know that you trust him and know that you are called to do his assignment. From there you go back to work and making the vision come to fruition.

God would not have given you life if you had no purpose of being here. Your life is precious and is necessary for the help of motivating others to stay alive and to keep believing in themselves and their dreams and visions that God has given them. This life is not just about you. This life is about others who need you. They need for you to declare that you are not a victim but a victor. That you are not unstable but stable. That you are not doubtful but hopeful. God needs for you to rise and let the enemy know that you are not going anywhere. You are not moving from your assignment because YOU ARE CAPABLE.

OBSERVATION:

Take time to think of how you view yourself. Do you see yourself as being able to do whatever you put your mind to? Do you often start something and not finish it? Do you find that doubt has the tendency to stop you from completing projects/ assignments? I am reminded of the story of Peter who had faith to walk on water. As Peter was walking, he began to see the strong wind and waves which began to terrify him causing his faith to waver and his body to sink. Jesus then asks him, "Why did you doubt?" (Matthew 14:28-31). This is a rebound question that I will ask you, why did you doubt? Why are you doubting yourself? Perhaps you are doubting yourself because of circumstances or conditions that are surrounding you today or perhaps it has to deal with your past. Either case, you know the answer. Think about it. Look at your life and see what it is saying about who you are in the area of being CAPABLE.

PETITION:
Dear Lord,

You are king! Forgive me for not always believing that I am capable. Thank you for letting me know that I am capable. Help me to remember each day that I AM CAPABLE.

In Jesus' name, Amen.

D.R.O.P. #29

You Are...

RELATABLE

DEFINITION:

RELATE: (*verb-used with object*) to tell; give an account of (an event, circumstance, etc.); to bring into or establish association, connection, or relation.

REFLECTION:

Have you ever been in a room full of people and felt like you were not able to connect with anyone? I know I have. And to be honest, I do not know if I felt this way because I was too timid to speak with anyone or if I honestly felt like no one could relate to me. Sometimes we may find ourselves pre-judging our ability to relate with others due to their outward appearance. You see the other person wearing nice clothes while you are wearing shrubs or they have a beautiful diamond ring while you are wearing a band and you then begin to think to yourself that there is no need to even approach them because they are out of your league or vice versa. You may be the one with fancy clothes and an outstanding ring and think that you wouldn't dare approach the lowly person because they are beneath your standards of who you would ever associate yourself with. But the truth is no one is greater or lesser than the other. We are all created equal by God with a need for relationships.

Genesis 2:18 reads, " Then the Lord God said, "It is not good for the man to be alone. I will make a helper who is just right for him." This scripture speaks of God creating Eve for Adam but I believe that it goes beyond just husband and wife. It speaks to the fact that God knows that we all need help. We need one another to help us progress in life. We need one another to help us press on when we feel like giving up. We need one another to help us get out of the pit that we dug ourselves into. We need one another to remind us that we are not in this life alone. We need one another because we need help.

We all will need help one day. If we do not need help today, then we will need help tomorrow or the day after tomorrow.

Whatever day it may be you can guarantee that all of our futures predict that we will need help. Ecclesiastes 4:10 reads, "If either of them falls down, one can help the other up. But pity anyone who falls and has no one to help them up." How tragic would it be for you to fall down, lose your strength to rise on your own and no one be around to help you get up? That would be horrible. And if you have been there before, then you can testify that having someone around to speak life into you during your worst days would have been helpful through that season. Once again, we need one another.

We will all have that time in our lives where we are tested and tempted. And during those times we need to be reminded that we are not the only ones who are going through this or who have been through it. 1 Corinthians 10:13 reads, "The temptations in your life are no different from what others experience. And God is faithful. He will not allow the temptation to be more than you can stand. When you are tempted, he will show you a way out so that you can endure." Sometimes you need someone to help you exit the door that God has given you to escape temptation. Sometimes you need someone to remind you of how far you have come to now turn back into your old bondage ways. Sometimes you need to admit that you do not have it all together and that you need a helping hand.

God sends his help to us by way of people. But how can we accept help from others if we are unwilling to associate and get to know one another? The help that you need for your business idea, broken marriage, difficult children, finances, etc. is all in your reach if you would just take time to speak to others and be honest in the areas that you may need assistance. In the end that is what relationships are for—to help. So before you decide to pass on speaking to someone because of their outer appearance or your insecurity remember that you may be the answer that they need and/or vice versa. There is no need to hesitate. You need help. Your life story is what will bring others near you because YOU ARE RELATABLE.

OBSERVATION:
Take time to think of how you view yourself. Do you see yourself as one who others can relate to? Do you think that your life story is worth telling? Do you believe that God created you to be alone? Do you know that you are the answer to someone's problem? You are the help that someone needs. You are the person that someone can relate to which is why you have to get out of your shell and speak to others. At all times, however, be wise with who you get to know as you are not the answer to everyone's problem. The Bible speaks on being careful with who you associate yourself with as it could lead to

bad character. You need to know your area of weakness so that you will know who you can and cannot connect with at this time. Your time and energy is valuable so be wise and led by the Holy Spirit with who you are to form a relationship with if this is something you desire to do. Think about it. Look at your life and see what it is saying about who you are in the area of being RELATABLE.

PETITION:
Dear Lord,

You are amazing! Forgive me for not always believing that I am relatable. Thank you for letting me know that I am relatable. Help me to remember each day that I AM RELATABLE.

In Jesus' name, Amen.

D.R.O.P. #30

You Are...

HEARD

DEFINITION:

HEAR: (*verb-used with object*) to perceive by the ear; to listen to; give or pay attention to; to listen to with favor, assent, or compliance.

REFLECTION:

Communication is key. Do you agree? When it comes to any relationship if you are not able to communicate with one another, then the relationship tends to suffer. You will not find joy in a relationship that does not provide a safe place to understand one another through conversation. And conversation is necessary to exchange thoughts. If you are not able to exchange thoughts with one another, then you will never know what the other person is thinking. This is where people get tired in a relationship because you show that you are unhappy, but when they ask you how you are feeling you say that you are good. How confusing is that for both parties? You must be able to communicate because it is the only way that you will be able to express yourself and receive answers.

Believe it or not, you are worth being listened to because your thoughts are important. When someone cares about you, they want to know what you are thinking to see how they can better service you. This is exactly the heart of God. He wants to hear your voice just as much as you want to hear his voice. John 10:27 says, "My sheep listen to my voice; I know them, and they follow me." Jesus is saying that his people know his voice and in turn he knows their voice and they adhere to what he says. This is the result of communication. When you speak to one another you will begin to know each other's voice. Proof that you are listening is by acting on what you have just heard.

James 1:22-25 reads, "But don't just listen to God's word. You must do what it says. Otherwise, you are only fooling yourselves. For if you listen to the word and don't obey, it is like glancing at your face in a mirror. You see yourself, walk away, and forget what you look like. But if you look carefully into the perfect law that sets you free, and if you do what it says and don't forget what you heard, then God will bless you for doing it." Hearing and doing go hand in hand. If you say that you heard but do not put any action to it afterwards, then the thought is that you were not really listening or you are blatantly showing that you do not care what has been said.

One way of confirming that you heard what someone said is to repeat what they said back to them to make sure that you understood their words. Understanding what has been said is needed so there are no misinterpretations. Misinterpretation will lead to confusion and wrong actions and wrong actions will bring about division. This is why it is important to not move on something until you fully understand what is being communicated. This reminds me of the importance of meditation.

Meditating on the word of God will allow you to begin to understand what God is fully saying to you. Once you have a full understanding of what God is saying then you can begin to put action to his word. Joshua 1:8 says, "Study this Book of Instruction continually. Meditate on it day and night so you will be sure to obey everything written in it. Only then will you prosper and succeed in all you do." Meditation will produce the desire to act upon what is being thought. This is why it is important to meditate on what is truly being communicated so that there is no room for error. When you act on what is truly being communicated then you will produce successful results.

Just as you desire for God to answer your prayers as proof of Him listening, God desires for you to obey his word to prove that you are listening. James 4:8 says, "Come close to God, and God will come close to you." This is the art of communication. Communication brings you close to one another. So take time to listen to others and others will take time to listen to you. Then what has been heard will begin to be acted upon. And remember, as a believer in Jesus Christ, you must believe that God hears your voice. So even if it takes days, months, years to see the manifestation of what you have prayed for, always remember that as a child of God YOU ARE HEARD.

OBSERVATION:

Take time to think of how you view yourself. When was the last time that you felt like you were heard? Do you ever feel like no one cares what you think or have to say? Are you moved by what you see? Does what you see cause you to feel like God is not listening to your prayers? Rest assured that God hears your voice. You have a voice that is worth hearing. I am reminded of the story of Ishmael, Abraham's son through Hagar (Genesis 21). Abraham had to send Hagar and Ishmael away per Sarah's request and God's instruction. Through the journey Hagar had ran out of water and was sure that her son Ishmael was going to die of thirst. But she cried out to God and God responded. God sent his angel to let Hagar know that he heard Ishmael crying in the wilderness. The angel told Hagar that God would make sure that Ishmael will live on to create a nation of his descendants. God then opened Hagar's eyes to see a well full of water to preserve her and Ishmael. Do you believe that God will come through for you like he did for Hagar and Ishmael? Are you worried about your circumstance? Think about it. Look at your life and see what it is saying about who you are in the area of being HEARD.

PETITION:
Dear Lord,

You are triumphant! Forgive me for not always believing that I am heard. Thank you for letting me know that I am heard. Help me to remember each day that I AM HEARD.

In Jesus' name, Amen.

D.R.O.P. #31

You Are...

KNOWN

DEFINITIONS:

KNOWN: (*verb*) past participle of know.

KNOW: (*verb-used with object*) to perceive or understand as fact or truth; to apprehend clearly and with certainty; to have established or fixed in the mind or memory; to be cognizant or aware of; be acquainted with (a thing, place, person, etc.) as by sight, experience, or report; to be able to distinguish, as one from another.

REFLECTION:

There's this song titled "Known" by Christian artist Tauren Wells. I remember hearing this song for the first time and I absolutely loved it (primarily because Tauren's voice is so smooth in sound.) Anyway, I did not fully know the words until I decided to look them up on the internet so that I could sing along properly, and to my surprise he was saying that he was "fully known." I thought at first he was saying "fully loved" but I was completely wrong, yet at the same time completely right. When I began to reflect on the idea of being fully known by God, I thought to myself how amazing our God is to know the ins and outs of us and still fully love us unconditionally.

1 Corinthians 13:4-7 reads, "Love is patient and kind. Love is not jealous or boastful or proud or rude. It does not demand its own way. It is not irritable, and it keeps no record of being wronged. It does not rejoice about injustice but rejoices whenever the truth wins out. Love never gives up, never loses faith, is always hopeful, and endures through every circumstance." Wow. Talk about big shoes to fill in when it comes to walking in love. But this is what God is to us, and this is what we must be to others. Even though we know that those who we are to love do not deserve it.

Deserve means that you have qualified to receive something due to your actions. Whether it's a reward or punishment, you will receive it because your actions have warranted that result.

Galatians 6:8 reads, "Those who live only to satisfy their own sinful nature will harvest decay and death from that sinful nature. But those who live to please the Spirit will harvest everlasting life from the Spirit." This is an example of "getting what you deserve." There is always reciprocation for your actions. You give love, you receive love. You show yourself friendly, you receive friendships. You forgive others, God will forgive you. The list continues. But there is an exception to this rule: unconditional love.

As we read in 1 Corinthians 13, we found that love is to be unconditional. You cannot say that you fully love someone unless you are able to carry out the flow of love that God has given us to follow. So if someone is rude to you, then that does not authorize you to be rude back to that person. Instead, you have to show them love. The Bible speaks about killing your enemy with kindness. When they are thirsty, give them a drink. When they are hungry, give them food. He does not authorize you to show hatred to those who hate you. That is not his heart and that is not his character. God's nature is to love you even though he fully knows you have not been the most lovable.

Let us keep it honest with one another. You are not "perfect." I am not perfect. We are not perfect. Each of us are a work in progress striving toward the perfection of his image and likeness. God knows everything about us. He knows our thoughts. He knows our past. He knows our present. He knows our future. He knows our temptations. He knows our shortcomings. He knows our secrets. He knows our fears. He knows our insecurities. He knows our concerns. He knows our sorrows. He knows our desires. He knows our strengths. God knows us. And with all that he knows, he still chooses to love us every time. He even set a new covenant with us that proved his love even deeper. Hebrews 8:12 reads, "And I will forgive their wickedness, and I will never again remember their sins." How awesome is our God? He has chosen to pardon our sins and no longer remember them. He has chosen to walk in love and keep no record of our wrongs. Of course this requires us to first confess our sins and repent for what we have done but after that we must rest in knowing that God no longer remembers ours sins even though you or others may still bring them up.

The human tendency to regurgitate sin is common to man because the enemy does not want you to forget what you have done to yourself and others or what others have done to you. He would love for you to stay in a place of stagnation by living a life of guilt, shame, unforgiveness and regret. This is why God desires that you resist temptation so that the enemy will flee and sin will not have its way in you. Practiced sin has the right to breed death inside of you, and death can only be shaken by the power of God who is able to mend your heart and revive you once again. For God knows that pardoning your sin is one thing but helping you to overcome the temptation to do it again or helping you move from self-turmoil is another thing that must be given much guidance and attention. But thanks be to God, he has already prepared a way for you by the way of Jesus Christ and the Holy Spirit who are here to help you through the process. And during this process you will be loved on because love will help you to endure. God knows exactly what you need to make it through this life. He loves you. He acknowledges you. YOU ARE KNOWN.

OBSERVATION:

Take time to think of how you view yourself. Have you ever become frightened at the thought of what others would think about you if they really knew you and what you have done? Have you ever felt like you were the only person that you could trust with your sin secrets? Do you find yourself feeling like you do not deserve to be loved by God or anyone else? 1 John 1:9 reads, "But if we confess our sins to him, he is faithful and just to forgive us our sins and to cleanse us from all wickedness." As stated before, God loves you unconditionally. He loves you tremendously and still desires to love you even after you confess your sins. He wants you to be washed clean from your sins so that you can move forward and fulfill your assignment in life. So even if others write you off for things you have done to them, know that God has not forgotten about you. He will not forsake you. You are still someone that He keeps in mind at all times. You are still someone that Jesus prays for daily. You are still someone that the Holy Spirit wants to help, guide and comfort. You are still someone who God acknowledges and loves. Do you believe this to be true? Think about it. Look at your life and see what it is saying about who you are in the area of being KNOWN.

PETITION:
Dear Lord,

You are gracious! Forgive me for not always believing that I am known. Thank you for letting me know that I am known. Help me to remember each day that I AM KNOWN.

In Jesus' name, Amen.